Decoding Instagram Mastery

Advanced Tactics for Influence and Engagement

23 chapters to Master Instagram

Guru Thilak

Guru Thilak is a seasoned marketing expert with over two decades of experience in digital marketing, branding, events, and promotions for top-tier brands. His immersion in the digital landscape began in 2011, propelling him to pursue continuous learning, mastery, and the passionate dissemination of his expertise. This book stands as a testament to his commitment to sharing invaluable insights, specifically tailored to harnessing the power of Instagram.

CONTENTS

CONTENTS

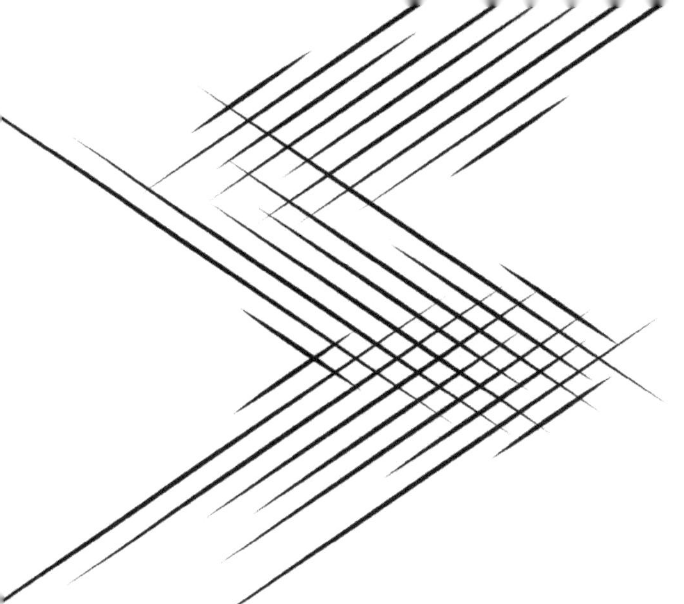

Viral Reels Strategy:

Mastering Content for Better Followers and Engagement

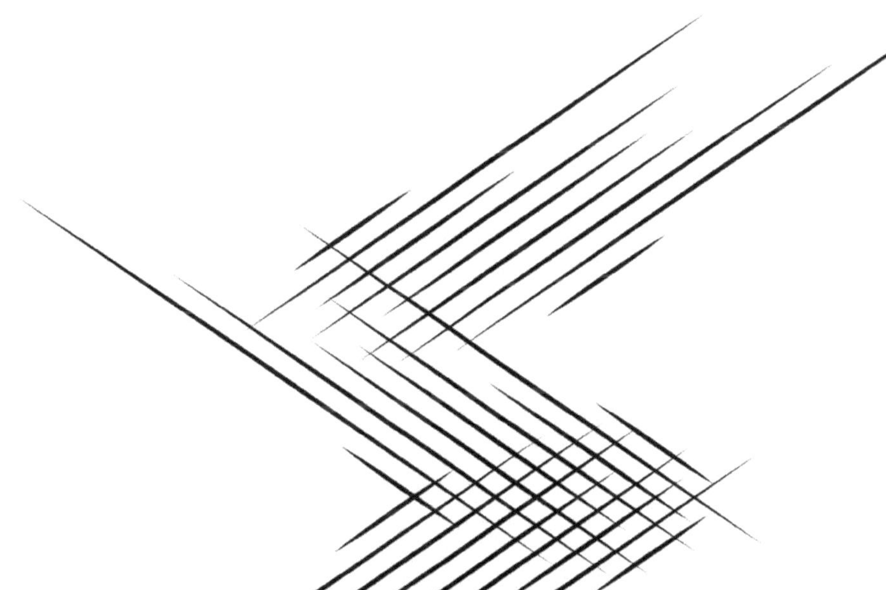

Proven Strategies for Success

Striven to prove the best out of 1000 brands
Through extensive work with entrepreneurs and influencers, I've refined strategies that not only worked for me but have been rigorously tested and proven effective across diverse niches. These strategies turn dreams into reality. When you implement them, success is inevitable.

Implement and Succeed

Try to implement the brilliant strategies taught in this book to reach thousands of followers in no time!

I'm committed to supporting you every step of the way in growing and monetizing your Instagram presence. Don't hesitate to reach out via grtguru@gmail.com. After purchasing the book, dive in, implement the strategies, and share your progress. Your feedback helps tailor my guidance to your needs.

I recommend creating 5-10 reels using the strategies and frameworks provided in the course. It's a surefire way to maximize your efforts.

Why wait? Start Reeling!!

The Value of Time and Effort

Time is definitely an important factor to consider. But it's worth it! Today's Instagram is at its peak. Several accounts every day, and everyone on Instagram is trying hard to draw the audience's attention.

Success takes time and effort. It's not magic; it's logic. Implementing the right strategies at the right time with the right frameworks will yield the results you seek. Your dedication to growing and monetizing your Instagram account is crucial, and I'm here to guide you every step of the way.

Key Takeaways

Things to Remember:
- Your first reel is just the beginning.
- Don't expect viral success from your first attempt.
- Aim to post one reel daily.
- Target 5 reels per week for 30 days.
- Allow 4-5 weeks to analyze what works best for you.
- Stay updated with trending videos and understand your audience's preferences.

Your first reel won't go viral overnight. It's a process of refinement. Stay consistent, posting daily and targeting at least 5 reels per week. It takes time—around 4-5 weeks—to discern what resonates best with your audience. Adapt your content strategy based on trends and audience feedback to maximize engagement.

Plan and create compelling content that captivates your audience effortlessly. Tune into your audience's preferences and adapt accordingly for sustained growth.

This revised content aims to inspire and guide aspiring influencers and marketers on leveraging Instagram Reels effectively, fostering growth, and maximizing engagement.

Introduction to Viral Reels Strategy

Welcome to the "Viral Reels Strategy" guide. If you're looking to grow your followers and enhance your content, follow this strategic framework to make your Instagram Reels captivating and effective.

The Hook-Value-CTA Framework

1. Hook (First 3 Seconds)

Your first task is to capture your audience's attention within the initial 3 seconds of your video. This is crucial as it determines whether viewers will continue watching or scroll past your Reel.

2. Value (Content Expertise)

Showcase your expertise by delivering valuable content specifically tailored for your audience. This establishes you as a subject matter expert and keeps viewers engaged.

3. Call to Action (CTA)
End every Reel with a clear and compelling call to action. Encourage your audience to like, comment, share, or follow. An effective CTA drives engagement and directs your audience on what to do next.

Understanding Instagram's Algorithm
To maximize the reach of your Reels, familiarize yourself with Instagram's algorithm, which prioritizes content based on:

- Engagement: Likes, comments, shares, and saves.
- Watch Time: How long viewers watch your Reel.
- User Interaction: How users interact with your previous content.

Encourage viewers to engage with your Reels by asking questions, seeking opinions, and creating interactive CTA captions. This will enhance your visibility on the platform.

The 4-Step Process to Analyzing Viral Reels
Once your Reels start going viral, follow these four steps to optimize your strategy:

1. Analyze Your Followers
Begin by studying your followers to understand their demographics and behaviors. Use Instagram Insights to gather data on who is engaging with your content.

2. Identify Success Patterns

If your followers are similar, pinpoint what aspects of your content are resonating well. This could be specific themes, styles, or formats that your audience loves.

3. Understand Audience Variation

If your viral Reels attract a different set of audiences, analyze why and how this happened. Understanding these nuances will help you diversify your content to appeal to broader demographics.

4. Replicate with Variation

Recreate successful content with a fresh twist. If a particular transition or style captivated your audience, experiment with new variations of the same concept to keep your content exciting and engaging.

Keeping Reels Fresh and Engaging

By following this framework and continuously analyzing your Reels' performance, you can create content that not only captures attention but also fosters a loyal and engaged following. Keep experimenting, stay informed about the latest trends, and always prioritize delivering value to your audience. Happy creating!

All You Need to Know About Reels:
Mastering Instagram's Viral Video Format

The Power of Understanding

Before diving into the mechanics of creating Reels, it's crucial to understand their essence. Grasping the fundamentals of Reels equates to comprehensive learning. The deeper your understanding, the more effectively you can leverage Reels to enhance your performance and engagement on Instagram.

Understanding Reels

Reels are short videos ranging from 15-30 seconds, though some accounts can create up to 60-second Reels. They offer a dynamic way to entertain and communicate with your audience.

- **Connection Through Interests:** The key to engaging your community is aligning your content with their interests.
- **Optimal Length:** While Reels can be longer, most successful ones are around 8-10 seconds. Shorter Reels are often more effective in capturing and maintaining audience attention.

Insight: Reels that fail to grab attention quickly, especially within the first 3-5 seconds, risk being overlooked as users swipe to find more engaging content.

Capturing Attention

The first 3-5 seconds of your Reel are critical. If you don't succeed in capturing your audience's attention quickly, they are likely to move on, which can negatively impact your account's visibility. Instagram favors content that keeps users engaged and on the platform longer.

Pro Tip: Ensure your Reels start with a bang to hook viewers instantly.

Why Reels Fail

Reels need to be concise and engaging. Long, drawn-out videos can bore viewers and cause them to lose interest.
- Crisp and Clear Content: Aim for clarity and brevity.
- Engagement in Seconds: Your goal is to connect with your audience within the first few seconds.

Pro Tip: Understanding your audience's preferences is essential for creating engaging content.

Seamless Transitions and Watch Time

Smooth and quick transitions are vital. Delayed transitions can lead to viewers skipping your Reel in favor of shorter, more engaging ones.

Faster Transitions: Keep transitions quick to maintain engagement.

Loop Videos: Shorter Reels often get watched multiple times, increasing overall watch time.

Insight: The more engaging and seamless your transitions, the more likely viewers are to stay and watch repeatedly.

The Reach of Reels

Reels are designed to reach a wide audience quickly, making them ideal for discovery and engagement.

Insight: In today's digital landscape, Reels are a powerful tool to connect with your ideal audience and expand your reach.

Instagram's Favoritism

Instagram continuously drives new audiences to trending content through features like:

- The Explorer page
- The Reel Explorer page
- Hashtags
- Trending audio
- Effects
- Suggested Reels section
- Facebook integration

Pro Tip: Leveraging these features can significantly enhance your content's visibility.

The Benefits of Reels

Reels offer numerous advantages:

- **Ease of Creation**: Reels are straightforward to produce.
- **Multi-Platform Sharing**: They can be shared across various platforms.
- **Unique Expression**: Reels allow you to showcase your personality and brand uniquely.
- **Vast Audience Reach**: They help you connect with a broad audience and attract more followers.

Insight: Reels enable a more personal connection with your audience, fostering trust and engagement.

Understanding Your Audience

Creating Reels that resonate with your audience is key. By understanding their preferences, you can tailor your content to captivate even those unfamiliar with you.

Pro Tip: Regularly analyze your audience's interests and adjust your content strategy accordingly.

Becoming a Subject Matter Expert

A subject matter expert produces content that meets the specific needs of their audience. Whether you're focusing on a brand or a business, expertise is crucial.

Pro Tip: Demonstrate your skills, knowledge, and expertise through your Reels to establish authority in your niche.

Showcasing Your Expertise

Create Reels that highlight:

- Your skills
- Your personality
- Your brand
- Your capabilities
- Your knowledge
- Your expertise

Insight: Video content is more memorable than text, making Reels a powerful tool for showcasing your talents.

Reels for Discoverability

Reels are excellent for building a community on Instagram. No account has failed by using Reels effectively.

Pro Tip: Consistently create and post Reels to attract and engage new audiences.

Prime Focus on New Audiences

When targeting new audiences, focus on:
- Discoverability
- Trending content
- Establishing authority

Pro Tip: Always aim to be seen as an authority in your subject to maximize visibility and engagement.

Essential Pro Tips for Publishing

When publishing your first Reel, remember to:
- Highlight your expertise
- Gain audience trust with original content
- Demonstrate why you're the best in your industry

Insight: Reels have a longer shelf life compared to other content. Be patient and allow your Reels time to gain traction

The Patience Game

Don't delete your Reels if they don't go viral immediately. Give them time to be discovered and shared.

Pro Tip: Sometimes, Reels gain popularity through the trickle-down effect, where the success of one boosts others.

By following these strategies and insights, you can master the art of creating engaging and viral Reels, ultimately growing your Instagram presence and connecting with a wider audience.

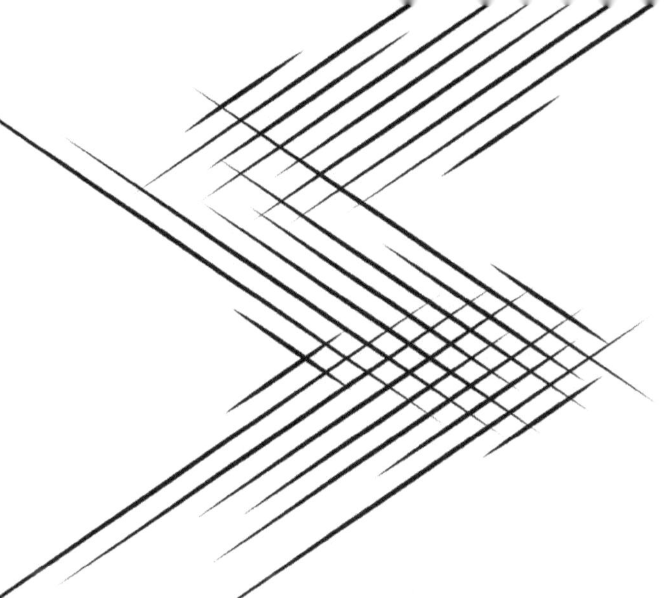

Road Map for Reels:

A Comprehensive Guide to Success on Instagram

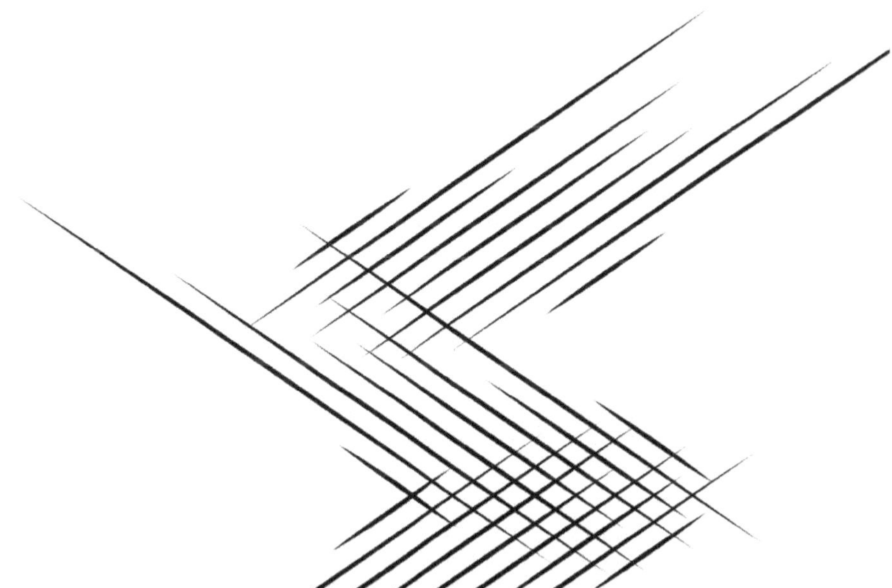

Road Map for Reels: A Comprehensive Guide to Success on Instagram

Research & Define Objectives

Before diving into creating Reels, it's essential to establish clear objectives. Understand the purpose behind using Instagram Reels. Are you aiming to:

- Increase brand awareness?
- Engage with your audience?
- Drive traffic to your website?
- Promote products or services?

Clarifying your goals will guide your content strategy and help you measure success.

Understand Your Audience

Identifying and understanding your target audience on Instagram is crucial. Consider their:

- Interests
- Preferences
- Behavior

This insight will enable you to create content that resonates deeply with them, fostering stronger connections and higher engagement.

Brainstorm Content & Ideas

With your objectives and audience in mind, brainstorm content ideas that align with both. Consider the types of content that perform well on Reels, such as:

- Tutorials
- Behind-the-scenes glimpses
- Challenges
- Entertaining videos

Innovative and relevant content ideas will keep your audience engaged and coming back for more.

Post Your Video

Creating high-quality, visually appealing videos is key. Focus on elements like:

- Lighting
- Sound
- Video editing

Utilize tools and effects, including audio and music, to make your Reels stand out. High production value can significantly enhance viewer engagement.

Engage

Engagement is vital. Interact with your audience through your videos by:

- Prompting responses
- Asking questions
- Encouraging likes, comments, and shares

Active engagement fosters a community and increases the likelihood of your Reels being shared.

Analyze

After posting 5 to 7 Reels, analyze their performance. Pay attention to:

- Number of likes
- Reach and views
- Viewer feedback

Identify which Reels are performing well and which are not. Understanding why certain content resonates more can help you refine your strategy.

Key Points to Note

Create Relevant Content: Ensure your Reels are engaging and align with trending concepts.

Use Effective Hashtags: Leverage viral hashtags to boost discoverability.

Consistency is Key: Post at least one Reel per day for 30 days to maintain a consistent presence.

Engage in Comments: Foster relationships by engaging with followers and audiences in the comment section.

High-Quality Content: Always strive to produce content that resonates with your audience.

Remember, your views are a measure of success. If your Reels aren't converting views, investigate and address potential issues in your account strategy immediately.

By following this road map, you can effectively harness the power of Instagram Reels to achieve your marketing objectives, engage your audience, and grow your brand.

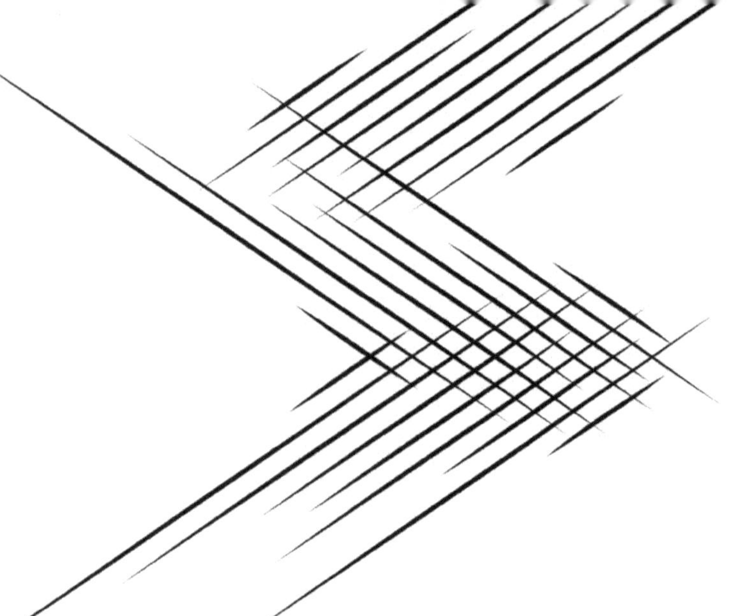

Best Toolkit to Make
Your Reels the Best!

Best Toolkit to Make Your Reels the Best!

The Importance of Lighting

Ring Light

Starting your Reels with proper lighting can significantly enhance their appeal. A ring light, in particular, can make a notable difference compared to regular lighting. One highly recommended option is the YOTZI LED Ring Light, which is both affordable and efficient. This product includes a 10-inch ring light and a 7-foot tripod, compatible with smartphones that can rotate 360 degrees. Such versatility ensures your Reels are well-lit and visually striking.

Creating the Perfect Backdrop

Backdrop Photo Light Studio

A backdrop can transform the look and feel of your Reels, making them more professional and engaging. While not every Reel requires a backdrop, having one on hand can be beneficial for certain types of content. One excellent choice is the Shopee Branded 8×1 FT Black Lekera Backdrop Photo Light Studio. This backdrop is affordable and provides a clean, polished background that can enhance the visual quality of your videos.

Enhancing with LED Room Lights

LED Room Lights

To add an extra layer of attractiveness to your Reels, LED room lights are a must-have. These lights are popular for providing additional illumination and creating a captivating atmosphere. A trending product in this category is the XERGY USB LED Strip Light, which comes with a mini controller for easy adjustments and is highly compatible with various setups.

Achieving Stability with Adjustable Tripods

Adjustable Tripod

For flexibility and ease of recording, an adjustable tripod is essential. It allows you to shoot from various angles and ensures stability during filming. The Digitek DTR455 LT is an excellent choice, offering reliability and ease of use. With this tripod, you can capture smooth and professional-looking Reels anywhere, anytime.

Ensuring Clear Audio with a Good Microphone

A Good Microphone
Clear audio is crucial for voice-overs and overall audio quality in your Reels. A high-quality microphone ensures that your voice is heard clearly, enhancing the overall effectiveness of your content. The JBL Omnidirectional Lavaliere Microphone is perfect for content creation, providing excellent audio clarity and ease of use.

By incorporating these tools into your Reels production setup, you can significantly improve the quality and appeal of your content. Each tool serves a specific purpose, from lighting and backdrop creation to stability and audio clarity, ensuring that your Reels stand out and captivate your audience.

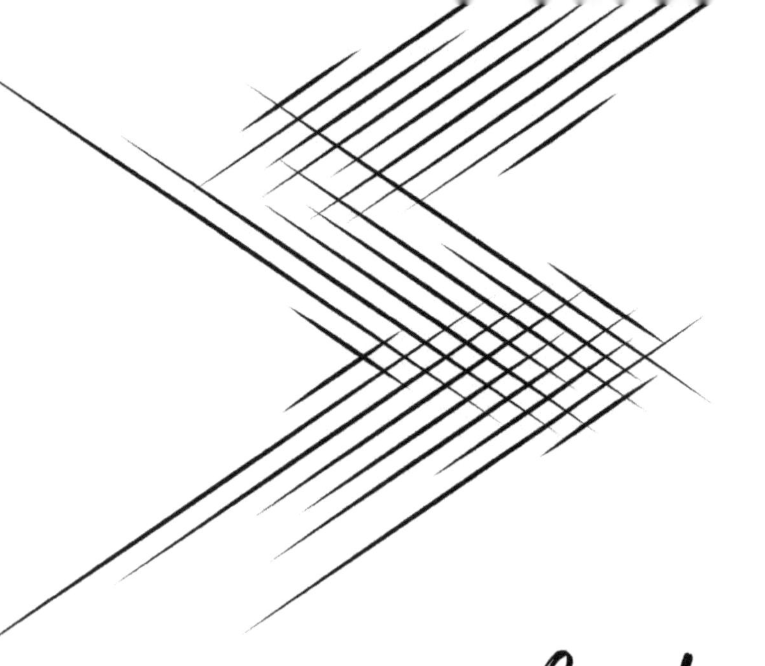

Content Strategy

Introduction to Content Strategy

Introduction to Content Strategy

Welcome to another session on content strategy. Having a solid content strategy is crucial for your success on Instagram Reels.

Consistency in Content

Audiences can get confused if your content is all over the place. If you post about makeup one day, dancing the next, and a music tutorial the day after, your audience won't know what to expect. They may see you as a jack-of-all-trades but a master of none, leading to a loss of interest and followers.

In the past, creators posted diverse content, but today, with nearly a billion users on Instagram, audiences prefer following experts in specific niches.

Focus on Your Unique Talent

Each person excels in one unique area. Your goal is to establish yourself as an expert in that field. By consistently posting valuable content related to your niche, your brand will become top-of-mind for audiences interested in that topic.

Example of a Consistent Content Plan

Let's imagine you specialize in skincare products:
Day 1: Showcase a skincare routine using your products.
Day 2: Share the story behind starting your business and your experience in the field.
Day 3: Highlight the advantages of using your skincare products.
Day 4: Provide tips on the correct and incorrect ways to follow a skincare routine.
Day 5: Discuss the importance of skincare in daily life.

This approach keeps your content focused and valuable.

Establishing Your Brand Focus

Concentrate on what your brand represents, understand its value, and focus on one niche where you are an expert. This clarity helps your audience easily identify and remember your brand.

Building Recognition

When you consistently provide valuable content, your audience will recognize you for your niche. They will remember your brand and trust you as an expert. Gradually, you'll receive messages with questions and queries related to your niche, indicating that your audience sees you as an authority.

Becoming Famous for Your Expertise

To grow your followers and monetize your content, you need to be known for your expertise in one area. For example, if you are a makeup artist, focus on makeup-related content. Demonstrate your skills and create engaging Reels that showcase your expertise.

Creating Educational Content

Educational content is highly effective. For example, if you focus on makeup, you could:
- Teach MUA hacks.
- Share your daily workout routine.
- Explain why you chose to become a makeup artist.
- Highlight the benefits of being an MUA.
- Discuss your professional experience.

Such content not only educates but also engages your audience.

Avoiding Distractions

Avoid using language or vernacular speech that only a specific audience understands. Keep your content simple and focused on your audience's needs.

The Secret to Engaging Content

Create content that's about your audience and less about you. Audiences love content that provides value and benefits them.

Example of Effective Content

For instance, a skincare brand could create a Reel titled "Four Steps to Make Your Skin Glow with Lavender Moisturizer." This type of content educates the audience on the product's benefits, making them more likely to purchase.

Example of Fashion Content

A fashion influencer might create a Reel on "Three Ways to Drape a Saree," while a beauty influencer could share "High-End Makeup Dupes." Such content is engaging and provides value to the audience.

Example of a Soap Factory

For a soap factory, you could create Reels on the do's and don'ts of using soaps, how your products differ from others, and the benefits of using organic soaps. Showcasing the production process and ingredients can make your content educational and interesting.

Key Points to Remember

Focus on creating simple, follower-centric content. Provide ideas on upcoming Reels and make your content easy to understand, even for a toddler.

Staying Consistent

Remember, you're just starting. You might gain or lose followers, but that's part of the journey. Stay consistent, engage with your audience, and provide valuable content. There are many people out there who need your expertise and will follow you for it.

By following these strategies, you can effectively use Instagram Reels to establish yourself as an expert in your niche, engage with your audience, and grow your brand

Mastering
Instagram Reels Algorithm

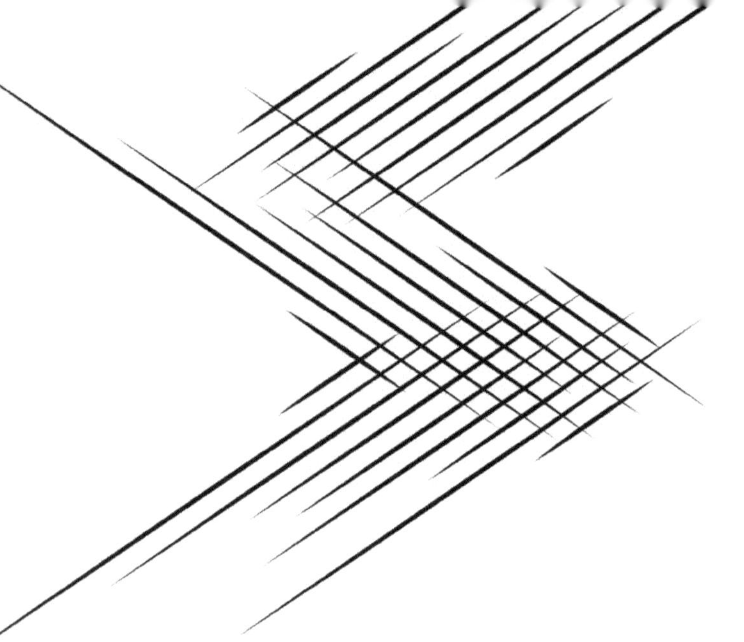

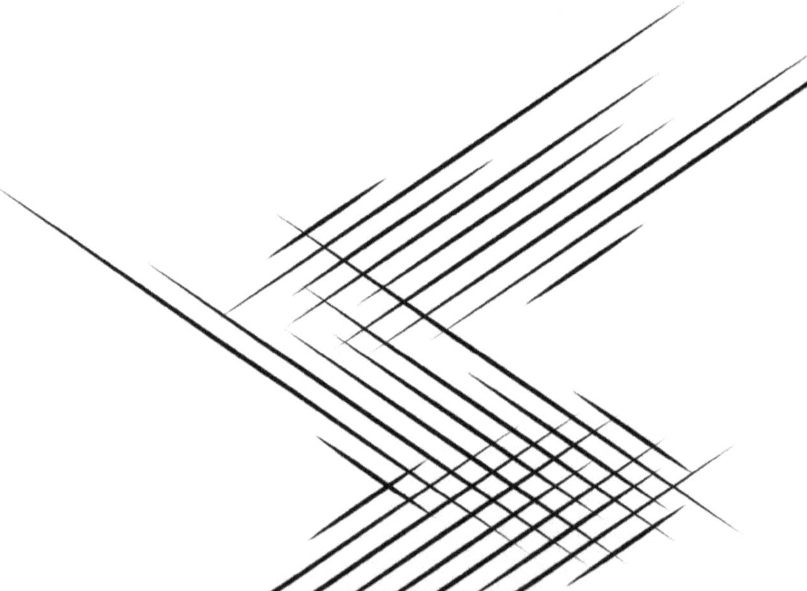

Understanding the Reach Dynamics

When you upload a Reel, it initially reaches a portion of your audience. As you engage with viewers, it gains visibility to a broader Instagram audience. This ripple effect of engagement is crucial for maximizing your reach.

Insights for Effective Engagement

Posting your Reels on both Instagram Feed and Facebook enhances visibility. Understand your audience's peak activity times and align your posting schedule accordingly. Utilize trending hashtags and keywords to capture broader attention.

Always monitor your insights to optimize your posting strategy. Engage actively with your audience; responding to comments and fostering conversations significantly boosts visibility. When someone engages positively, respond thoughtfully to encourage further interaction.

Engagement Hacks

Respond to comments on your Reels instead of just liking them. The next day, revisit your previous Reel and like all comments. This tactic triggers notifications, increasing the chances of your Reel appearing on their feed again.

Instagram prioritizes content that keeps users engaged. Avoid using watermarks or logos that aren't yours, as they can limit your reach. Experiment with different features and transitions for engaging content.

Recommended Reels Creation Apps

Here are some recommended apps for creating engaging Reels:

- Power Director
- Promeo
- Inshot
- KineMaster
- Splice
- Final Cut Pro

Explore these and other apps to find the one that best suits your creative needs. Remember, Instagram offers robust tools to create compelling Reels directly within the app.

By understanding and leveraging the Instagram Reels algorithm, you can strategically enhance your visibility and engagement, ultimately growing your presence on the platform.

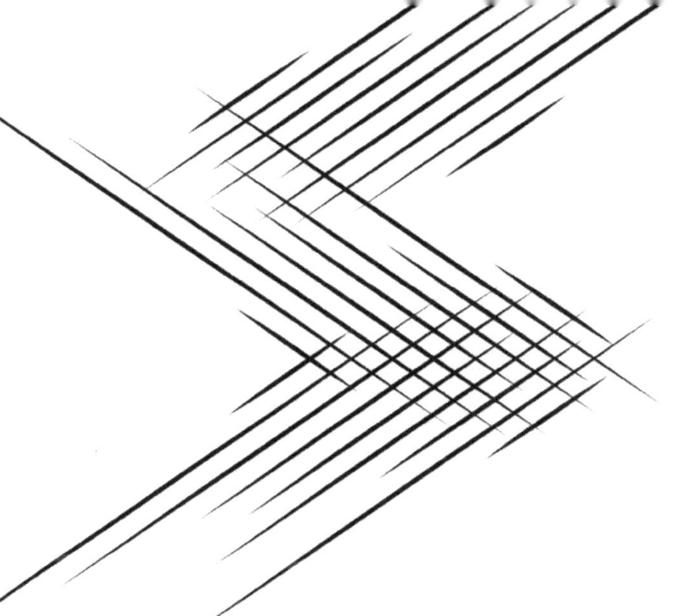

Mastering Product/Service-based
Business on Instagram

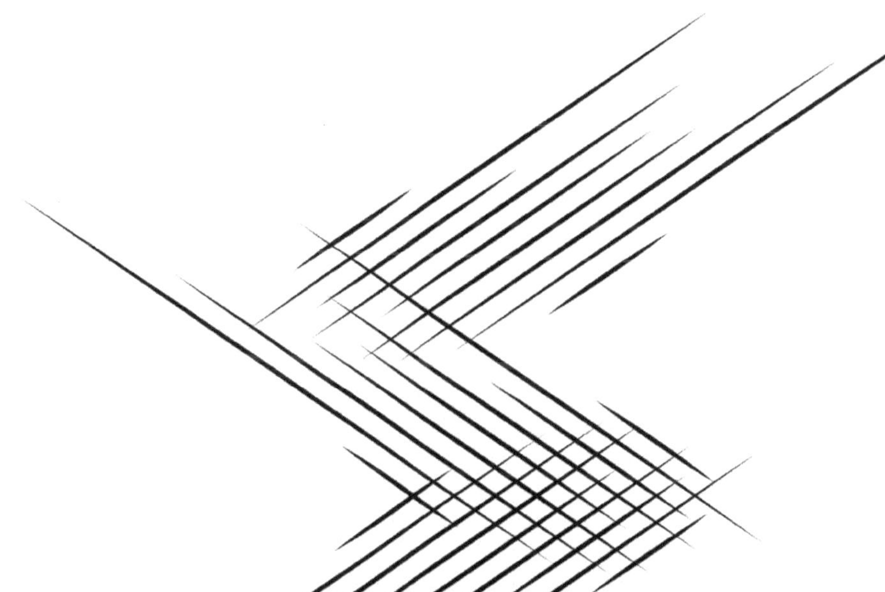

Mastering Product/Service-based Business on Instagram

Welcome to this session where we dive deep into strategies for product/service-based businesses on Instagram. Whether you're an entrepreneur or a marketer, this session is crucial for anyone aiming to effectively promote their offerings.

As a product-based business, direct promotions can often backfire, leading to audience disengagement and potential unfollows. Instead of pushing sales, focus on creating Reels that resonate with your audience's interests and needs. By centering your content around them, you build a connection that enhances brand understanding and loyalty.

When your audience relates to your product, they're more likely to engage and initiate direct messages, seeking further interaction and understanding of your brand's values and offerings. Crafting meaningful Reels with a clear content strategy plays a pivotal role in capturing their attention.

Differentiating your product promotions from traditional sales pitches is key to capturing audience attention. For instance, rather than simply promoting candles, highlight them as "Perfect for a cozy candlelit dinner at home! Easy to use with a divine aroma." This approach sparks imagination and demonstrates how your product benefits their lifestyle.

Using compelling phrases and attention-grabbing tactics in your promotions is essential. Collaborating with influencers and businesses in your niche can broaden your reach and provide authentic endorsements, enhancing credibility.

Share stories about the inspiration behind your products or services, or how they've positively impacted customers. Emotional storytelling resonates deeply with audiences and builds a strong brand narrative.

Running Instagram giveaways or contests that require audience participation, such as tagging friends or sharing personal experiences, boosts engagement with your content and fosters a community around your brand.

Capitalize on holiday seasons and special occasions like Christmas or Diwali by creating unique Reels and content tailored to these events. Craft videos that resonate with your audience's celebration mood, making them feel your product is designed specifically for them.

When addressing discounts, transparently explain the limitations of small business margins. Authentic communication fosters trust and understanding among your audience, setting realistic expectations.

Certain months or holidays can significantly boost sales. For example, Halloween in the U.S. or Dussehra in India are prime opportunities to leverage festive spirits and capture attention towards your offerings.

Tailor your promotional strategies to target specific audience demographics such as gender, age, and locality. For instance, if promoting a skincare routine kit, highlight its benefits for those facing skincare challenges due to late-night work schedules.

Engage with your audience actively. Respond to queries, showcase customer testimonials, and interact with followers consistently. Instagram's algorithm favors content that generates engagement, ensuring your product remains visible to potential customers.

Create curiosity-driven Reels that gradually unveil your product's features and benefits over several days. This keeps followers intrigued and invested in your content, increasing their likelihood to convert into customers.

Let Instagram's algorithm work for you by implementing the strategies discussed in this session. By aligning with these tips and hacks, you can streamline your promotional efforts and effectively reach your target audience.

By strategically leveraging these insights and tactics, you can elevate your product/service-based business on Instagram, fostering meaningful connections and driving sustainable growth.

Unveiling Faceless Reels: Crafting Engaging Content
In this chapter, we delve into the art of creating captivating Faceless Reels. These ideas are designed to connect with your audience on a personal level while showcasing aspects of your daily life and business journey.

Share a Day in Your Normal Life:
Take your audience on a home tour, offering a glimpse into your personal sanctuary. Share the cozy corners, decor inspirations, and what makes your space uniquely yours. Engage your viewers by addressing them as part of your family, fostering a sense of belonging.

Capture your daily routine with enthusiasm, highlighting exciting moments and activities that bring joy to your day. Provide practical tips and ideas, such as natural gardening techniques or simple DIY projects, enriching your audience's lives through valuable insights. Inspire others with your positivity and happiness. Share moments that uplift and motivate, encouraging your viewers to find joy in the little things every day.

People are inherently curious about the routines of others. By inviting your audience into your daily life, you create a relatable connection that strengthens their bond with your content.

Share Your Workspace:
Take your audience on a tour of your workspace, whether it's a cozy home office or a bustling studio. Introduce them to your business environment and the passionate team behind your brand. Inspire them with the entrepreneurial journey that led to your business's inception.

Showcase the process of packing orders, revealing the dedication and care that goes into fulfilling customer requests. Tease your audience with sneak peeks of your next product launch, generating excitement and anticipation.

Engage directly with your audience by demonstrating your products or services. Use engaging beats and visuals to highlight the unique features and benefits of your offerings. Respond to positive comments and feedback, fostering a community around your brand.

Recycling your posts creatively can breathe new life into your content strategy. Convert your carousel images into standalone posts, reviving older content with fresh perspectives. Reflect on how your approach to content creation has evolved since your early days on Instagram, showing viewers the growth and learning that came with experience.

ocus on revisiting an old tutorial, updating it with current insights and techniques. Use your platform to educate and empower your audience, with at least five posts aimed at teaching positive skills or perspectives.

DIY (Do It Yourself) Videos:
Create engaging DIY videos that empower your audience to explore their creativity. Share step-by-step tutorials on crafts, home decor projects, or practical solutions using your products. Encourage viewers to unleash their inner creativity and share their creations with you.

By embracing these Faceless Reels ideas, you not only connect more deeply with your audience but also inspire and educate them through your personal and professional journey. Each reel becomes a window into your world, fostering a meaningful connection that transcends the screen.

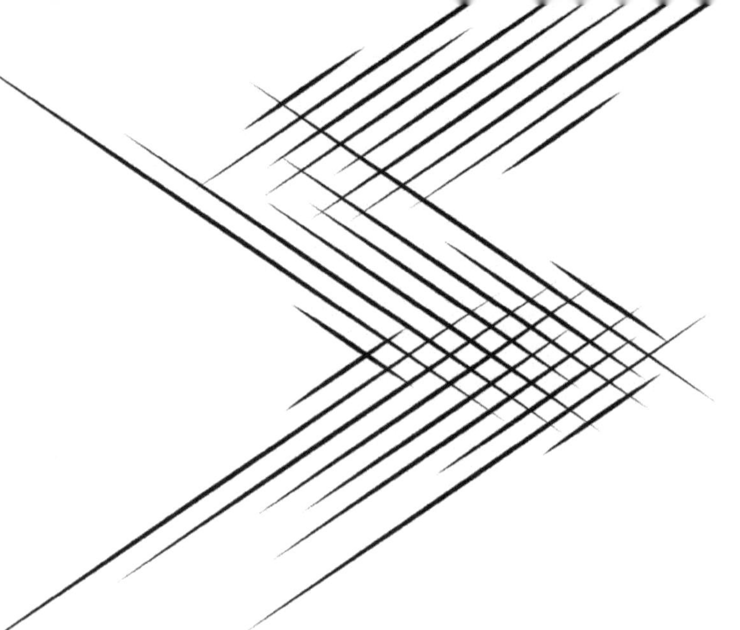

Innovative Reel Swaps:
Revolutionizing Product Advertisement

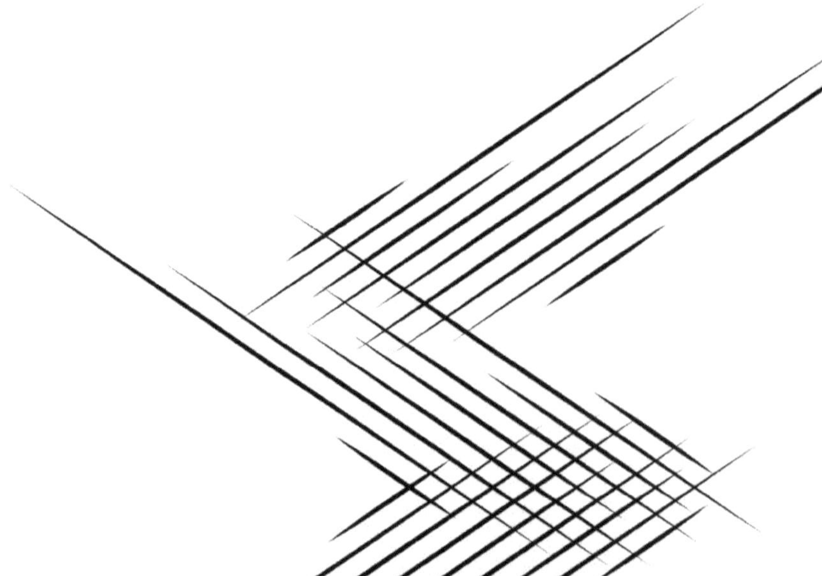

In this chapter, we explore innovative ways to advertise products using Reels, ensuring maximum engagement and impact. These strategies aim to captivate your audience's attention and leave a lasting impression through creative and effective messaging.

Product Advertisement:

When promoting a new product, move beyond traditional announcements to capture attention and build anticipation. Instead of simply stating "New product launching soon," entice your audience with the immediate benefits they can expect. For example, highlight the transformative effects of your face wash with a compelling statement like, "Searching for a face wash that brightens in just 2 minutes?" Conclude with a teaser: "Stay tuned for the super product launching soon!" This approach not only intrigues your audience but also encourages repeated visits to your page in anticipation of the release.

Advertising a Book or Journal:

Transform the way you advertise books or journals by appealing to aspirations and personal growth. Rather than a straightforward call to action like "Buy our journal or book," inspire your audience with a New Year resolution theme. Say, "Embark on a journey to discover a new you this New Year!" This approach not only promotes your product but also aligns it with personal goals and aspirations, making it more appealing and relatable.

Best Ways to Advertise Your Product via Reels:

Introduce Your Brand & You:
Establish a strong brand identity by introducing your brand's values, uniqueness, and personal story. Engage your audience by showcasing what sets your brand apart from competitors, building trust and recognition.

Introduce Your Product:
Highlight your product's key features and benefits using trendy phrases and captivating visuals. Make your product essential in your audience's mind by presenting it in a way that resonates with current trends and preferences.

Introduce Your Team:
Highlight the dedication and expertise of your team members who contribute to your product's success. Showcase their efforts and commitment, fostering trust and credibility among your audience.

Brief Your Work Culture:
Offer transparency by sharing insights into your work culture, from packaging and shipping processes to daily operations. This behind-the-scenes look allows your audience to connect on a deeper level, reinforcing their loyalty to your brand.

Tell Your Brand Story & How It All Started:
Use Reels to narrate your brand's journey, employing creative transitions and effects to engage a wide audience. Share the inspirations and challenges that shaped your brand, creating an emotional connection with viewers.

Reel Your Customers' Experiences:
Highlight genuine customer testimonials and experiences to build credibility and trust. Showcase how your product has positively impacted customers' lives, encouraging others to explore your brand. Encourage interaction by prompting viewers to tag friends and family who might benefit from your products.

By implementing these innovative Reel swaps, you not only promote your products effectively but also cultivate a loyal and engaged audience eager to connect with your brand's story and offerings. Each Reel becomes an opportunity to inspire, empower, and build lasting relationships with your customers.

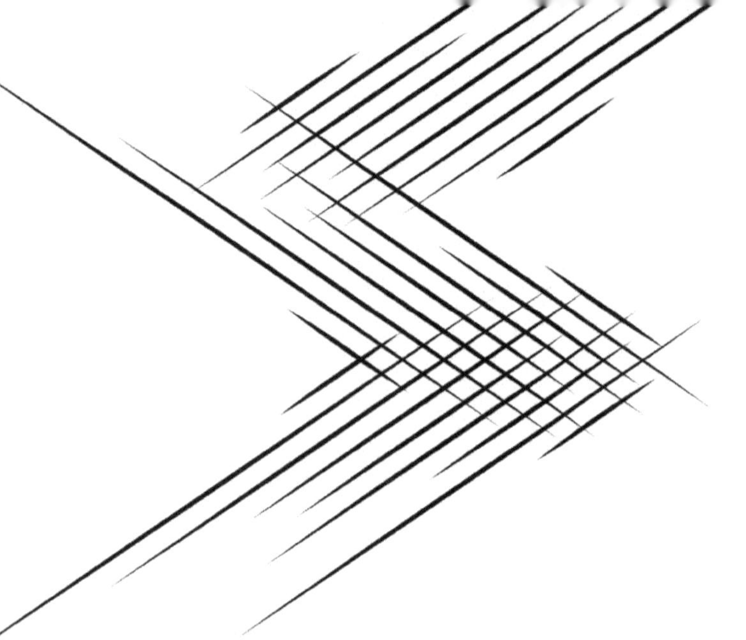

Content Ideas &
How to Utilize Them Effectively

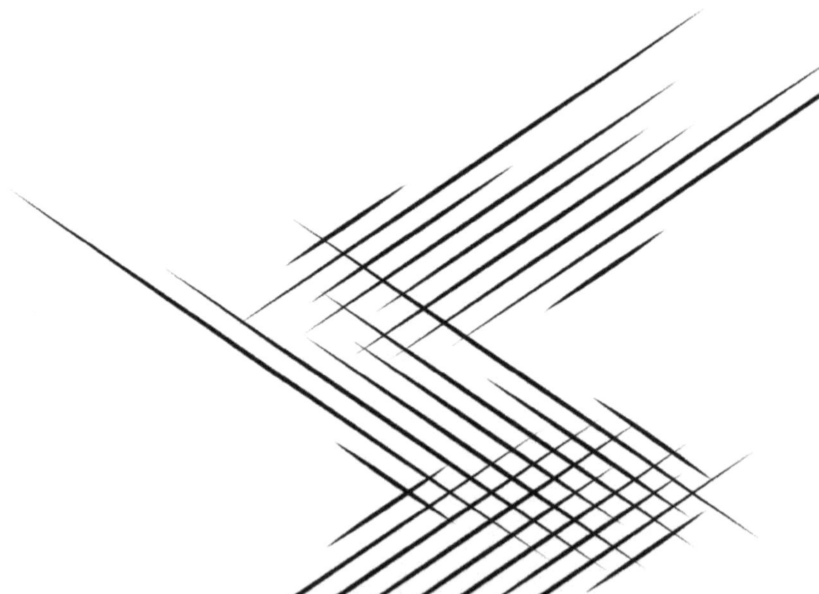

Content Ideas & How to Utilize Them Effectively

Displaying the Excel Sheet with Content Ideas

Welcome to Module 26, where we dive into 130 content ideas designed to elevate your social media strategy. I recommend downloading the Excel sheet available in the download section. While you can't edit this original, you can make a copy for yourself by navigating to the "Files" menu or simply download it.

Before delving into customization, consider your ideal audience. Why haven't they followed you yet? Reflect on how you can showcase your expertise and passion within your niche. This step is crucial for brands aiming to forge new connections through engaging content, particularly using Reels. Remember, your content should never resemble a sales catalog, as this can deter interest. Instead, use Reels to highlight your uniqueness among peers.

Now, let's discuss how you can tailor these ideas to suit your brand. Notice the column labeled "Status of the Reels to be Created," alongside "Tracking the Reels with Views/Likes/Comments." Tracking your efforts from the outset is essential for gauging progress. By month's end, you'll easily evaluate your growth and adjust strategies accordingly.

For example, let's take the first idea, "My Go-To Product." If your focus is on makeup, showcase essential products like brushes or makeup items. If you're in sports, highlight equipment pivotal for peak performance, such as stable cricket gear. For jewelry brands, feature organizational tips for preserving precious items in vanity boxes.

Next, consider "Podcast" as a content idea. Suppose you're a skincare expert or a vegan beauty influencer. Utilize Reels to discuss insights from recent podcasts about the benefits of vegan skincare. Alternatively, draw from recent research, articles, or insights shared by industry experts or celebrities.

Similarly, as a fashion influencer, use Reels to articulate why sustainable fashion is crucial, drawing from magazines or journals. Position yourself as a subject matter expert, ensuring followers perceive you as knowledgeable within your niche.

By leveraging these tailored content ideas effectively, you not only engage your audience authentically but also establish credibility and deepen connections within your community. Each Reel becomes a platform to showcase expertise and build a loyal following eager to engage with your unique insights and offerings.

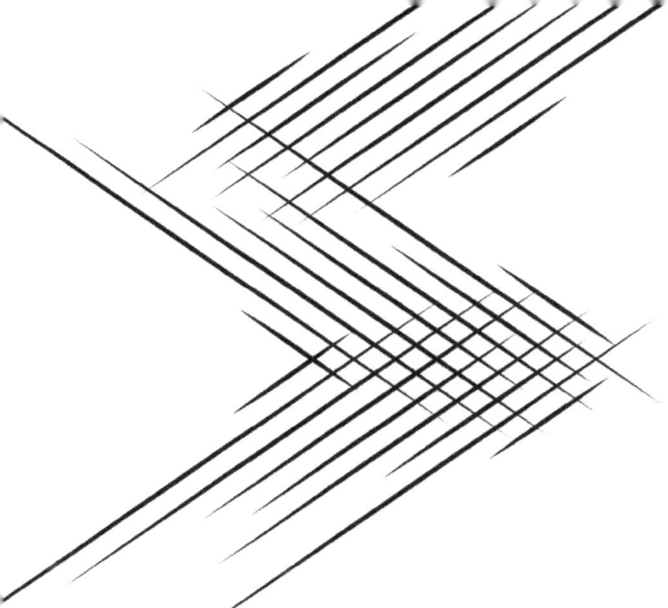

Mastering Instagram Reels:

A Step-by-Step Guide

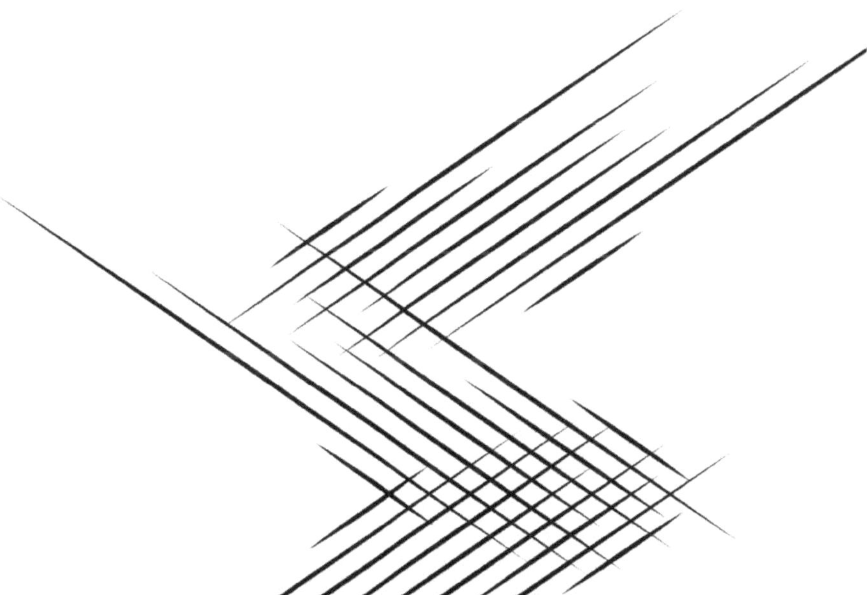

Mastering Instagram Reels: A Step-by-Step Guide
Welcome to the ultimate guide on mastering Instagram Reels! Whether you're new to creating content or looking to refine your skills, this chapter will walk you through everything you need to know—from uploading videos to adding engaging elements like music and transitions. Let's dive in!

How to Post a Reel – Tutorial
1. Accessing Reels: Open Instagram Stories and tap the Reels button located at the bottom of the screen.

2. Uploading a Video:
  - Tap "Upload Video" and select the video from your camera folder.
  - Use editing tools to trim the video, add music, and apply filters.

3. Recording a Reel:
  - Tap the camera button at the bottom left to record up to 30-second clips.
  - Use editing tools to add filters, effects, and adjust speed.

4. Adding Text:
  - After uploading or recording a video, tap "Next," then the "Text" icon.
  - Add static text or dynamic text that moves across the screen.

5. Adding Music/Audio:
   - Tap the music icon to add music from Instagram's library or use audio from other Reels.
   - Adjust the volume and select portions of the song using the slider.

6. Creating Multi-Clip Videos:
   - Use the timer to record multiple clips with effects.
   - Alternatively, manually start and pause recording for each segment.

7. Transitions:
   - Use a self-timer to film actions, trim to key moments, and use the align tool for seamless transitions.
   - Experiment with basic to advanced transitions for engaging content.

8. Publishing Your Reel:
   - Tap "Next" to write a caption, add up to 30 hashtags, and tag users.
   - Share directly to Reels feed or Instagram feed, or save as a draft.

9. Adding a Cover Photo:
   - Choose a cover image that fits your feed aesthetic from your camera roll or create one using design tools like Canva.
   - Align the subject centrally for aesthetic consistency.

Viewing Reels

Home Page: Scroll down to see Reels from accounts you follow.

Friend's Page: Visit a friend's profile, tap the Reels icon, and scroll to view their Reels.

Explorer Page: Navigate to the Explorer page where Reels occupy prominent space. Click on Reels to explore more.

Search: Use hashtags to find Reels via the search function. Click on Reels to view posts.

Mastering Instagram Reels opens up endless possibilities for creative expression and audience engagement. Whether you're showcasing your talents or promoting a brand, these steps will guide you to create compelling content that captivates your audience. Start creating, experimenting, and watch your presence grow on Instagram Reels!

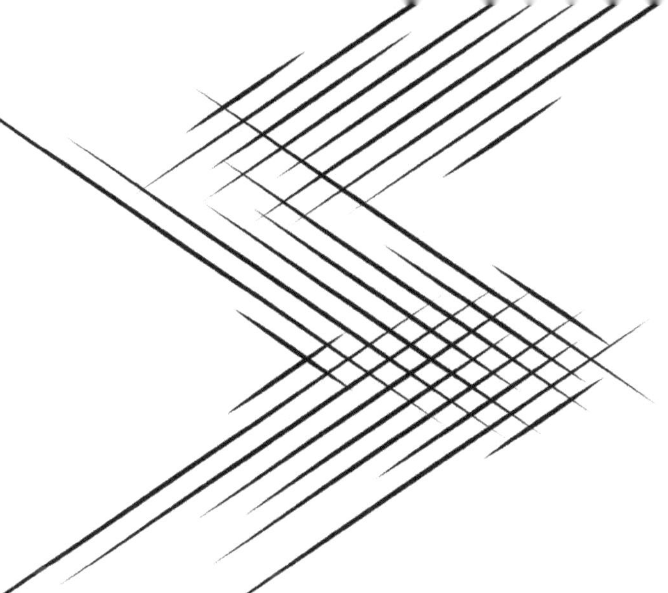

Mastering Instagram Growth:
How to Reach 10k Followers in 30 Days

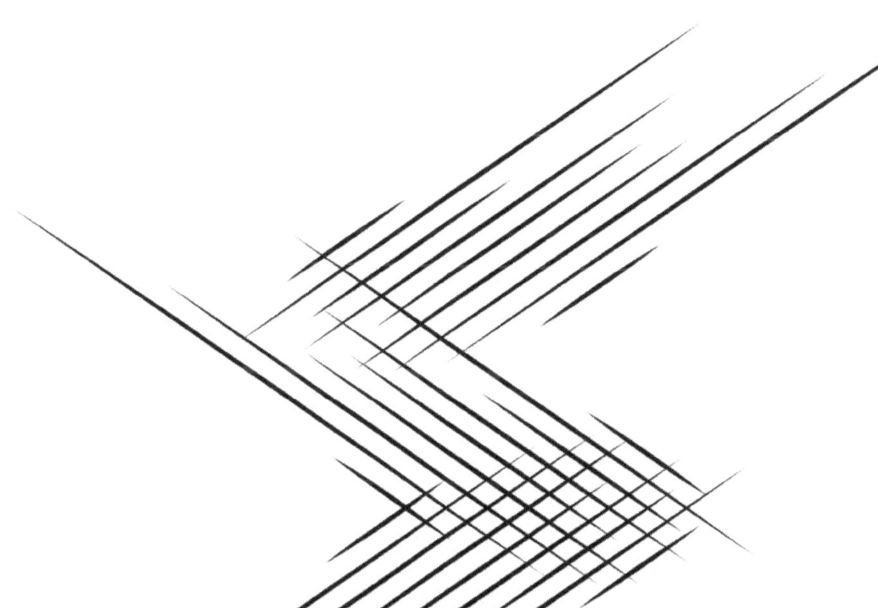

Mastering Instagram Growth: How to Reach 10k Followers in 30 Days

Welcome to the definitive guide on achieving 10,000 followers on Instagram in just 30 days! This chapter will equip you with actionable strategies and insights to turbocharge your follower growth. Let's dive into the step-by-step process to elevate your Instagram presence.

Guidelines to Grow 10k Followers

1. Consistent Reel Posting:
   - Post one Reel daily without fail to maintain engagement and visibility.

2. Optimize Posting Times:
   - Check your insights to identify the most active times of your audience.
   - Post your Reels during these peak periods for maximum visibility.

3. Content Strategy:
   - Focus your Reels on inspirational, trending, educational, and valuable topics that resonate with your audience.

4. Utilizing Insights:
   - Navigate to your profile and click on "Insights."
   - Under "Insights Overview," select "Total Followers" to view analytics.
   - Identify "Most Active Times" to schedule your posts strategically.

5. Diverse Reel Content:
   - Out of 30 Reels:
      - 10 Reels should feature trending audio and music.
      - 10 Reels should focus on evergreen or timeless content.
      - 5 Reels should convert your top-performing posts into video format.
      - 5 Reels should address frequently asked questions to provide value and engagement.

6. Captivating Captions:
   - Use trending and attention-grabbing captions to enhance engagement.
   - Include a powerful Call-to-Action (CTA) to prompt audience interaction.

7. Video Quality:
   - Ensure your Reels are high-quality with clear resolution and professional editing.

8. Unique Concept Development:
   - Experiment with fresh and original concepts to maintain audience interest.
   - Avoid repetition to keep your content exciting and engaging.

9. Hashtag Strategy:
   - Use at least 5 niche-specific hashtags relevant to your content.
   - Incorporate 5 hashtags directly related to each Reel.
   - Opt for mixed hashtags with a post range between 20,000 to 25,000 for optimal reach.

By implementing these proven strategies, you're equipped to accelerate your Instagram growth journey to reach 10,000 followers in just 30 days. Consistency, strategic planning, and engaging content will be your allies in achieving this milestone. Start applying these tactics today and watch your Instagram presence flourish!

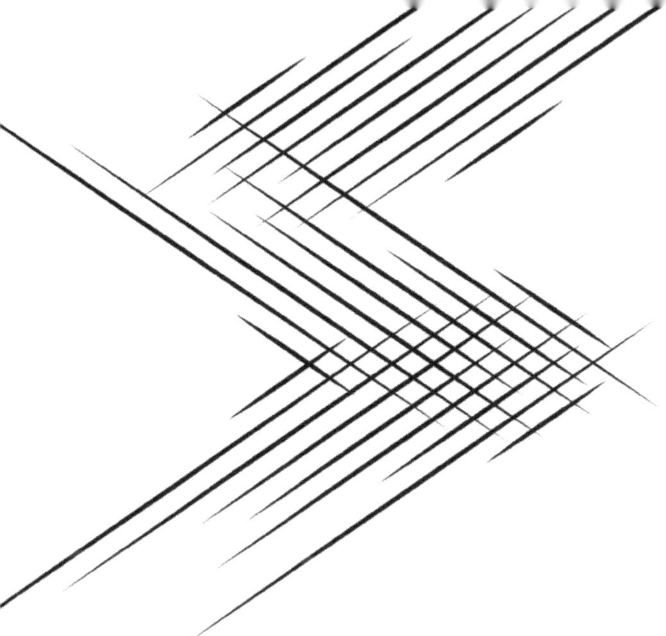

Optimizing Your Reels
for Maximum Engagement

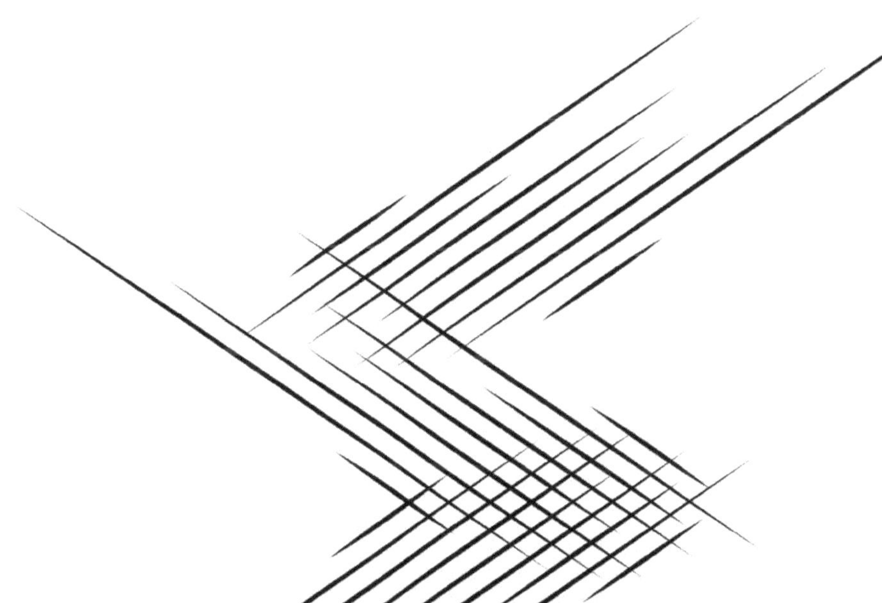

Optimizing Your Reels for Maximum Engagement

Welcome to the ultimate guide on fixing your Instagram Reels for maximum results! In this chapter, we'll address common issues faced by creators and provide actionable strategies to enhance your Reels' performance. Let's dive into transforming your content strategy for optimal engagement and growth.

When Views Don't Convert to Followers

Issue: Your Reels reach viewers but fail to convert them into followers, leading to follower attrition.

Solution: Optimize your Reels for better engagement by refining content quality and appeal. Identify gaps in your profile that might be deterring potential followers.

When Your Hashtags Aren't Effective

Issue: Hashtags used are not relevant or connected to your Reels, affecting discoverability.

Solution: Utilize a mix of short, relatable hashtags with higher chances of featuring. Experiment with both shorter and longer hashtags to broaden reach and visibility.

When Views Outpace Engagement (Comments/Likes)

Issue: Your Reels receive views but lack comments and likes, indicating passive viewership.

Solution: Craft compelling captions with strong Calls-to-Action (CTAs) and questions that provoke audience interaction and curiosity.

Low View Counts
Issue: Your Reels aren't attracting enough views despite being posted.
Solution: Ensure your Reels are of high-quality and provide substantial value to viewers. Post during peak active times to maximize notifications and engagement.

Not Appearing on the Explorer Page
Issue: Difficulty in getting featured on Instagram's Explorer Page.
Solution: Create visually appealing and engaging content that resonates with your target audience. Focus on current trends and topics to increase visibility and reach.

Standing Out Amongst Competition
Issue: Your Reels fail to stand out amidst a competitive landscape.
Solution: Stay updated with trending content and adapt your Reels accordingly. Explore diverse themes and styles to capture audience interest and differentiate yourself.

By implementing these strategies, you'll be equipped to optimize your Reels effectively and achieve maximum engagement on Instagram. Remember, consistency, quality, and audience connection are key to enhancing your presence and growing your follower base. Start refining your Reels today and watch your engagement soar!

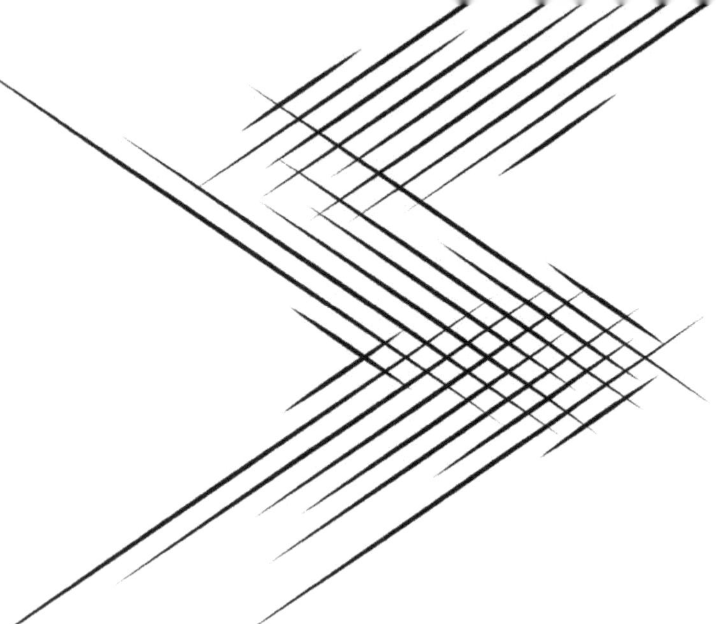

Mastering Trending
Audio for Reels

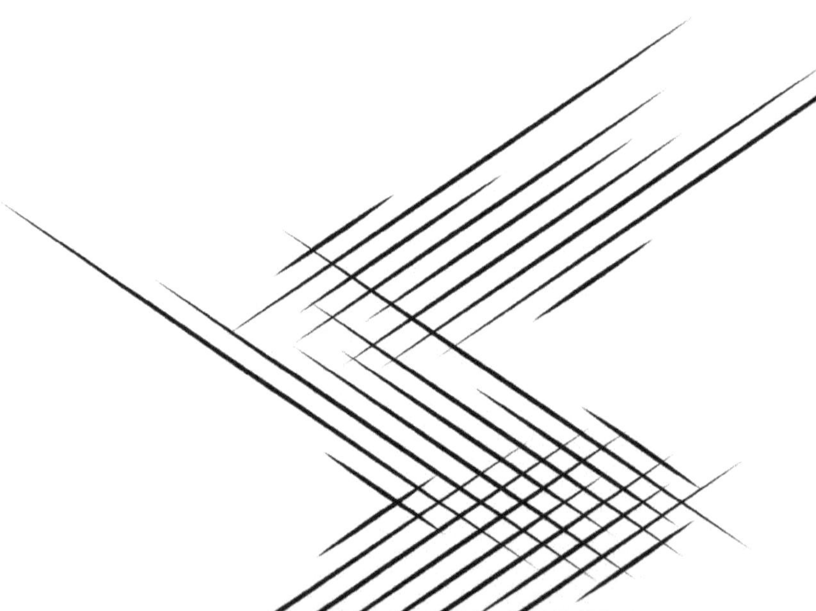

Mastering Trending Audio for Reels

Welcome to the definitive guide on finding and utilizing trending audio for Instagram Reels! In this chapter, we'll uncover the steps to identify popular music tracks and audio clips that can elevate your Reels' engagement and visibility. Let's dive into mastering the art of leveraging trending audio for maximum impact.

Step-by-Step Guide

1. Accessing Reels Section
   - Open your Instagram app and navigate to your profile.
    - Tap on the Reels icon in the lower navigation menu, resembling a small video camera.

2. Browsing Audio Tracks
    - Browse through the Reels feed to discover various audio tracks being used by creators.

3. Recording or Selecting Video
   - Record a new video by tapping the record button or select an existing video from your camera roll.

4. Adding Trending Audio
    - After recording or selecting the video, tap on the "Audio" icon located on the left-hand side of the screen.

5. Searching for Specific Audio

- Use the search bar at the top to search for specific audio or trending music tracks.

6. Exploring Featured Audio

- Scroll down to explore featured audio and trending music categories within the Reels editor.

7. Identifying Trending Audio

- Navigate to the Reels Explorer page and look for an upper-right arrow icon next to the audio track.
- If the arrow appears, it signifies that the audio is currently trending on Instagram.

8. Utilizing Trending Audio

- When creating batches of Reels, prioritize using the trending audio identified.
- Reels featuring trending songs have higher chances of gaining traction and potentially going viral.

By following these steps, you'll be equipped to seamlessly integrate trending audio into your Instagram Reels, enhancing their reach and engagement. Stay tuned to current trends and leverage popular music tracks to captivate your audience effectively. Start exploring trending audio today and elevate your Reels to new heights of engagement and visibility!

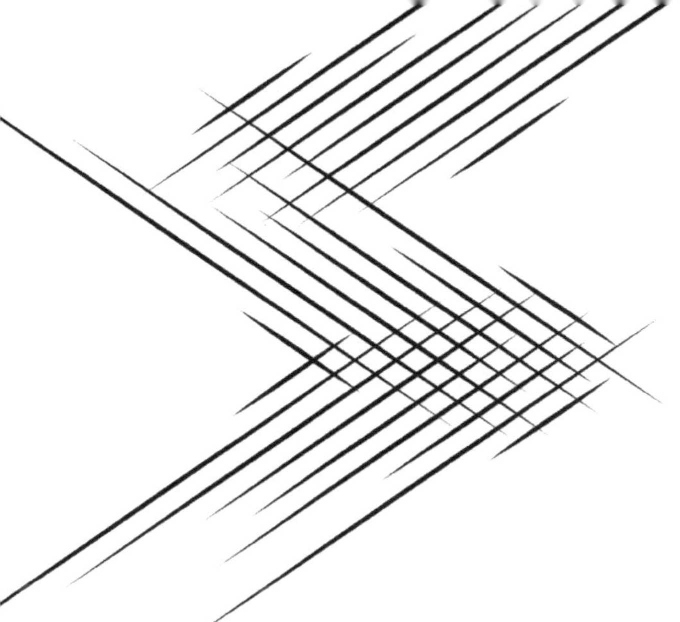

Unlimited Content Ideas
for Instagram Reels

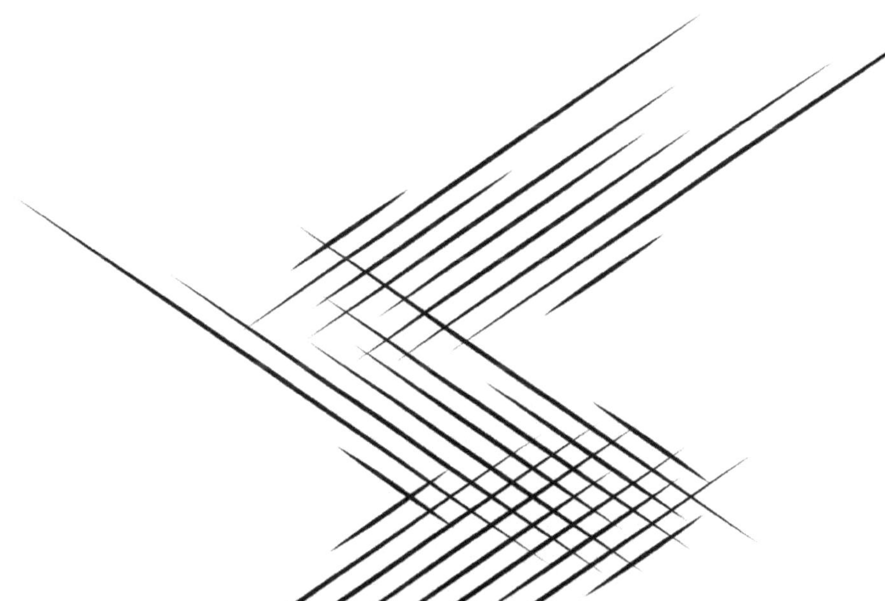

Unlimited Content Ideas for Instagram Reels

Welcome to the ultimate guide on generating endless content ideas for Instagram Reels. In this chapter, we'll explore foolproof strategies to ensure you never run out of engaging content ideas that resonate with your audience. Let's dive into the methods that will keep your content fresh and compelling.

Step-by-Step Guide

1. Leveraging Insights
- Start by understanding your audience's preferences and interests. Go to your Instagram profile and access Insights.
- Navigate to "Posts" and review metrics such as shares, saves, interactions, and follows over the last 6 months.
- Identify the top-performing Reels and analyze what content resonates most with your audience.

To kick off, let's delve into leveraging insights to understand your audience's preferences. By accessing Insights on your Instagram profile and exploring the "Posts" section, you can uncover which Reels have garnered the most shares, saves, interactions, and follows over the past six months. This data is invaluable for tailoring your content to meet your audience's expectations.

2. Recreating Top Performers
- Select the top three Reels that have performed exceptionally well in terms of engagement and reach.
- Use these Reels as inspiration to create new content that aligns with your style and adds a unique twist.

Once you've identified your top-performing Reels, consider recreating them in your own creative style. While maintaining the essence of what made these Reels successful, infuse them with your personal touch to captivate your audience anew.

FAQs
- Dive into your DMs and comments section to uncover frequently asked questions from your audience.
- If you're starting out or have a smaller following, draw inspiration from larger accounts in your niche.
- Create Reels that directly address these FAQs or host Q&A sessions to engage your audience actively.

Moving on to FAQs. Your audience is your best source of content ideas. Take a deep dive into your DMs and comments section to identify frequently asked questions. For those new or with smaller followings, look to prominent accounts in your niche for inspiration. Craft Reels that directly address these queries or consider hosting interactive Q&A sessions to foster engagement.

Engaging via Stories

- Utilize Instagram Stories to poll your audience on their preferences for future content.
- Incorporate interactive elements like polls, quizzes, or challenges to solicit input and gauge interest.
- Host live Q&A sessions to provide immediate responses to your audience's inquiries and deepen engagement.

Engaging through Instagram Stories offers a direct line to your audience's preferences. Use polls and other interactive features to gather insights into what content your followers are eager to see next. Additionally, consider hosting live Q&A sessions where you can address audience questions in real-time, fostering a deeper connection with your community.

Drawing Inspiration

- Seek inspiration from both large and small accounts within your niche.
- Avoid copying content directly; instead, adapt concepts and add your unique perspective.
- Explore diverse niches for fresh ideas that can be tailored to resonate with your audience's interests.

Another strategy is drawing inspiration from accounts within and beyond your niche. Take note of what works well for others but ensure your content remains authentic. Adapt ideas to fit your style and audience while exploring different niches for innovative approaches.

Keyword Research
- Use keyword tools to identify popular topics and questions related to your niche.
- Visit platforms like answerthepublic.com to discover frequently searched queries and topics.
- Tailor your Reels to address these keywords effectively, ensuring relevance and resonance with your audience.

Harness the power of keyword research to generate targeted content ideas. Utilize tools to uncover trending topics and questions within your niche. Platforms like answerthepublic.com are invaluable for discovering what your audience is searching for. Craft Reels that directly respond to these keywords to maximize relevance and engagement.

In conclusion, maintaining a steady stream of compelling content for Instagram Reels is achievable by tapping into audience insights, leveraging FAQs, engaging via Stories, drawing inspiration wisely, and conducting thorough keyword research. By aligning your content strategy with your audience's preferences and interests, you can consistently deliver content that resonates and drives engagement on Instagram. Keep listening to your audience and evolving your content strategy to stay ahead in the dynamic world of social media.

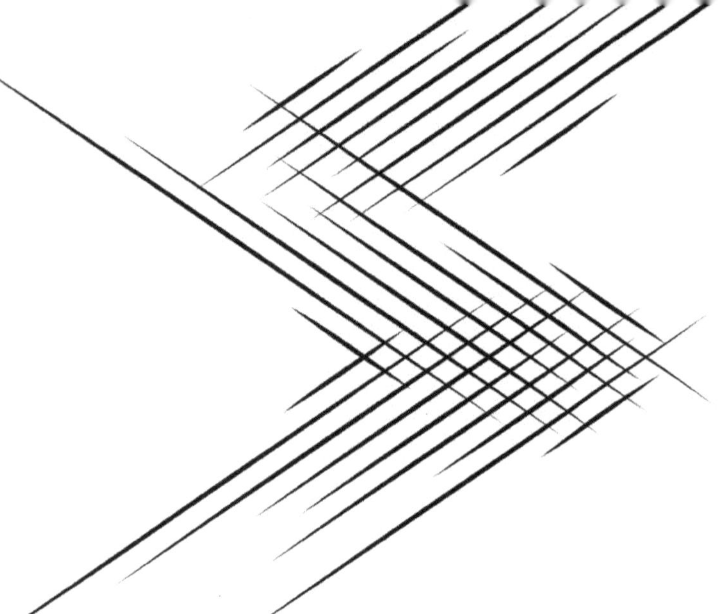

Evergreen Content Strategy
Content that works

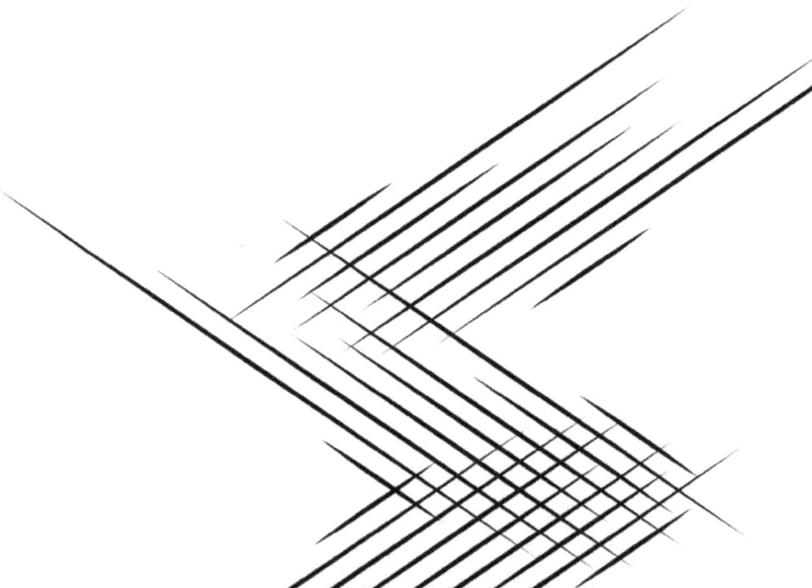

Evergreen Content Strategy

Evergreen Content

Welcome to the definitive guide on creating evergreen content that resonates with your audience and stands the test of time. In this chapter, we'll explore the importance of evergreen content and how to integrate it seamlessly into your content strategy.

When crafting content that stands the test of time, always consider what your audience truly desires and actively searches for. Evergreen content remains relevant long after its initial publication, making it a cornerstone of your content strategy. Here are some key strategies to create compelling evergreen content:

Informative and Educational Content:

- Share informative and educational content that addresses common problems or questions in your niche. These posts serve as invaluable resources for your followers.
- Create step-by-step guides and tutorials that provide practical solutions related to your industry or expertise. Evergreen tutorials offer lasting value to your audience.

Showcasing Products and Services:
- Highlight key features and benefits of your products or services. Illustrate how they solve specific problems or enhance the lives of your audience.
- Provide behind-the-scenes insights into your business or creative process. Stories about your team, workspace, or production methods humanize your brand.

Social Proof and Testimonials:
- Share success stories and testimonials from satisfied customers. This social proof reinforces the value and credibility of your offerings.

Expert Advice and Best Practices:
- Offer expert advice, top tips, and best practices within your industry. Such insights attract new followers seeking valuable information.

Frequently Asked Questions (FAQs):
- Compile a comprehensive list of FAQs and provide detailed answers in your posts. FAQs are evergreen as they address ongoing concerns within your community.

Historical and Milestone Content:
- Share interesting historical facts, anecdotes, or milestones relevant to your niche. Historical content often maintains its relevance over time.

Seasonal Adaptations:
- While some content may be tied to specific seasons or holidays, adapt it to have an evergreen appeal. For example, a holiday gift guide can transform into a general gift-giving guide.

Product Demonstrations:
- Regularly showcase how to use your products effectively or demonstrate their benefits. This helps potential customers understand the practical value your products offer.

Repurposing and Updating Content:
- Occasionally revisit and repurpose well-performing evergreen content from the past. Update it with fresh insights or perspectives to keep it relevant.

Interactive Content:
- Create interactive content such as quizzes, polls, or challenges that engage your audience and encourage participation. Interactive formats enhance user engagement and retention.

Educational Series:
- Develop a series of interconnected educational posts. Each post should stand alone while contributing to a broader educational theme, providing continuous value to your audience.

In conclusion, crafting evergreen content requires a deep understanding of your audience's needs and preferences. By focusing on timeless topics, practical solutions, and engaging formats, you can build a repository of content that remains relevant and valuable over an extended period. Embrace the power of evergreen content to strengthen your brand's authority, attract new followers, and foster lasting connections with your audience.

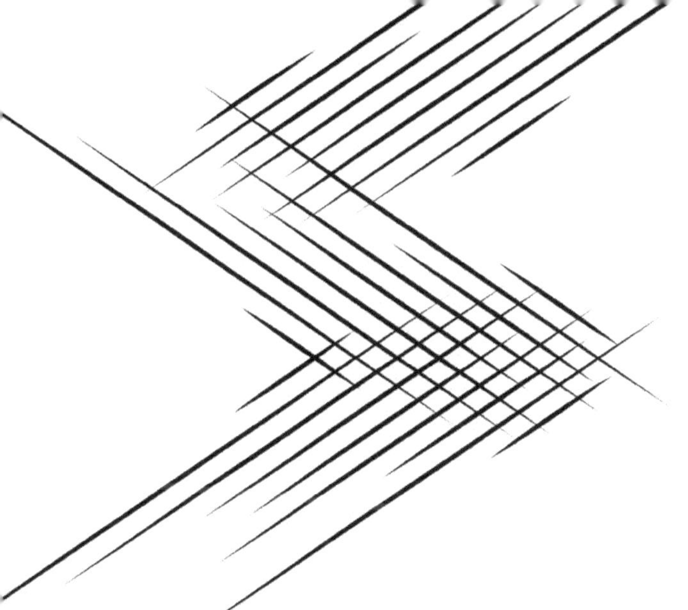

Enhancing Watch Time

on Instagram

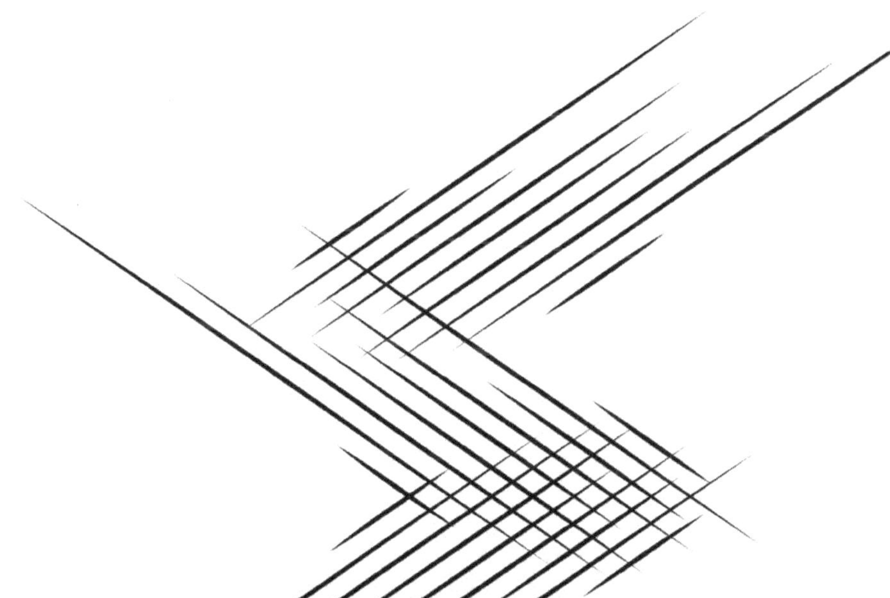

Enhancing Watch Time on Instagram

Increasing Watch Time

Welcome to the chapter on "Enhancing Watch Time" where we explore strategies to keep your audience engaged longer with your content. Remember, longer watch times signal strong content engagement and attract new audiences to your profile.

One effective way to boost watch time is by strategically using disappearing text. Incorporate text that disappears quickly in your reels or videos. This encourages viewers to rewatch the content multiple times to catch all the information. Educational content particularly benefits from this technique, as viewers pause and replay to absorb insights.

Shorter videos also play a crucial role in maximizing engagement. Audiences tend to prefer concise content that addresses their immediate interests or concerns. Short videos are more likely to go viral due to their quick consumption and high relevance. They also facilitate efficient content batching, allowing you to produce more content within a shorter timeframe.

To keep viewers engaged till the end, consider adding riddles or cliffhangers within your content. Pose a thought-provoking question or promise a surprising conclusion towards the end of your video. This creates anticipation and motivates viewers to stay till the end to uncover the answer. Some may even rewatch the video to fully understand the riddle, thus boosting your watch time metrics.

These strategies not only enhance viewer retention but also increase the likelihood of your content being recommended to new audiences by Instagram's algorithm. By implementing these techniques, you can effectively enhance watch time and drive sustained engagement on your Instagram reels and videos.

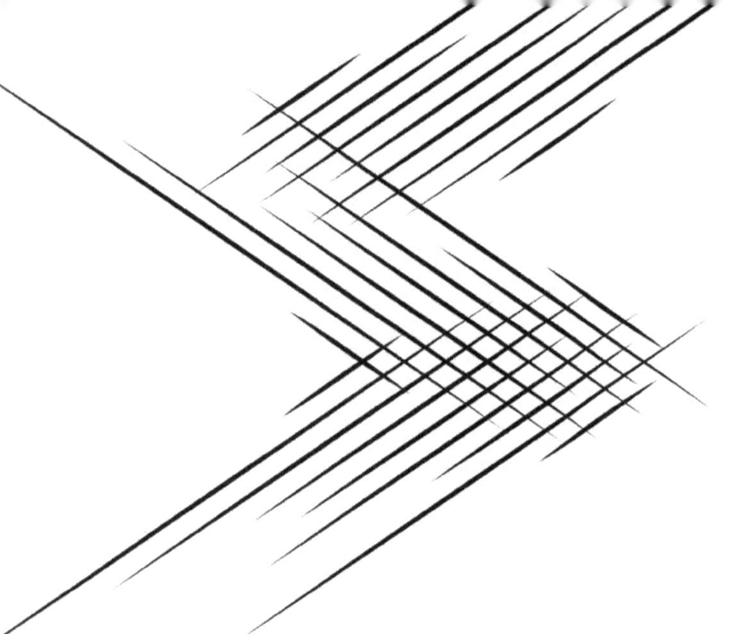

Content Strategies
for Reels

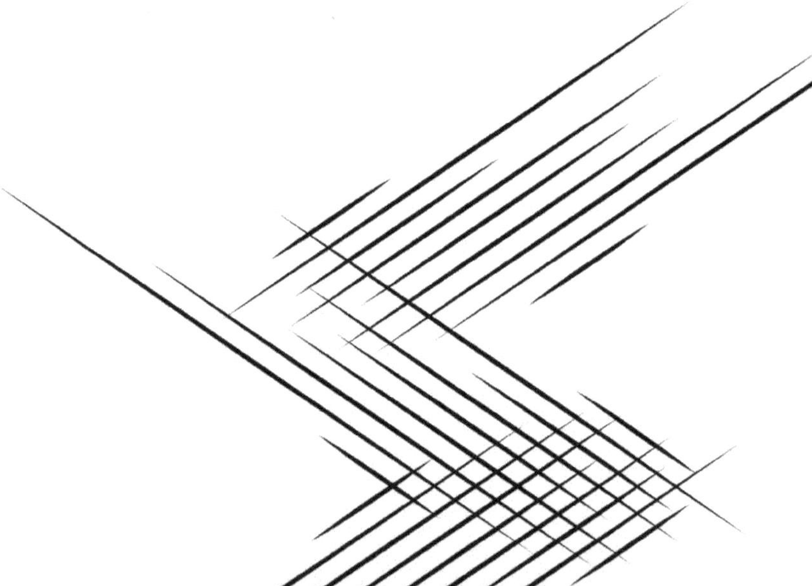

Content Strategies for Reels

Welcome back to the Content Strategies for Reels module! In this segment, we delve into the diverse types of content you can create to enhance engagement and reach on Instagram Reels.

Educational Content

Let's start with educational content. This type of content is highly effective across all niches on Instagram. Educational content involves sharing valuable insights, debunking myths, and teaching your audience something new. For instance, you can provide quick tips, hacks, or behind-the-scenes looks related to your niche. Educational quizzes and trivia games also engage audiences effectively.

Educational content not only boosts engagement but also positions you as an authority in your field. Take for example a makeup artist teaching how to apply winged eyeliner—a tutorial that not only demonstrates skill but also builds trust with potential clients.

Creating Value for Audiences

Content that provides real value to your audience has several benefits. It increases watch time, encourages saves for later viewing, and prompts shares with friends and family. High watch time signals to Instagram's algorithm that your content is engaging, potentially amplifying its reach to new audiences.

Examples of Educational Content

Let's explore examples tailored to different niches:
- Food Blogger: Recipe videos, cooking variations, kitchen tips.
- Skincare Brand: Skincare routines, product benefits, skincare tips.
- Photography: Tips on equipment, lighting techniques, photography styles.
- Pet Essentials: Grooming tips, pet care products, training advice.

Each example demonstrates how educational content can be tailored to educate and engage specific audiences effectively.

Consistent Posting

To maintain engagement, consistently post content that resonates with your audience. Address common queries from your DMs or comments, share personal stories, or highlight your journey in your niche. Authenticity and relatability are key to sustaining viewer interest.

Engaging Your Audience

Engage your audience by soliciting content ideas directly from them. Use Instagram features like polls, questions, or host challenges to encourage participation. By involving your audience in content creation, you foster a sense of community and increase overall engagement.

Strategies for Viral Reels

To create viral Reels, focus on creating visually captivating content with unique transitions and compelling narratives. Shorter videos tend to perform better, leveraging trending hashtags and encouraging viewer interaction through likes, shares, and comments.

Showcasing Your Brand

Reels offer a dynamic platform to showcase your brand's story, values, and products. Highlight the benefits of your offerings subtly through engaging content that resonates emotionally with your audience.

Highlighting Efforts and Impact

Demonstrate the effort behind your content creation, highlight the impact of your products or services, and showcase the tangible results. This builds credibility and reinforces your brand's value proposition effectively.

Being Unique in Your Niche

Your uniqueness sets you apart in a crowded digital landscape. Embrace your individuality by presenting content in your own style and voice. Don't shy away from exploring unconventional topics or formats that align with your brand's personality.

Polarizing Content

Polarizing content challenges common beliefs and sparks meaningful discussions. Use this strategy thoughtfully, ensuring you have well-researched facts and a clear perspective to share. It can attract attention and establish you as a thought leader in your niche.

Avoiding Common Pitfalls

Avoid the trap of directly copying content from larger accounts in your niche. Instead, identify gaps or unexplored topics and create content that is uniquely yours. Leverage your creativity and personal style to make a lasting impression on your audience.

As we conclude this module, remember to leverage educational content, engage your audience through interactive features, and maintain authenticity in your content creation. These strategies will not only enhance engagement but also establish your authority and expand your reach on Instagram Reels.

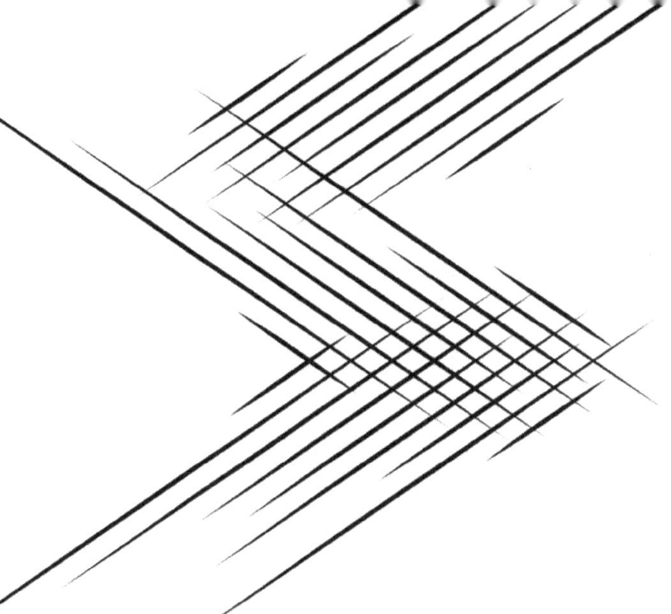

Captions

How to pick the right ones

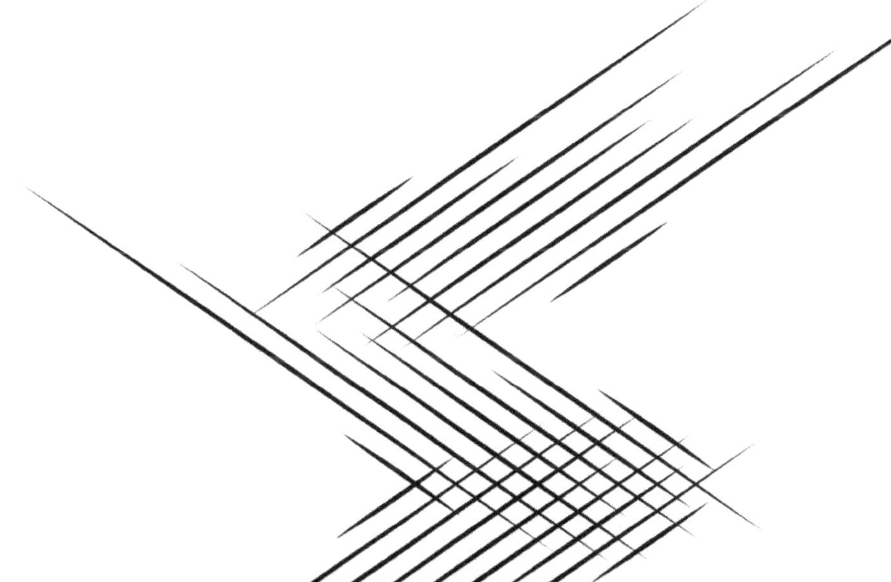

Captions

Welcome to the world of Instagram captions, where a few words can make a world of difference for your content. Crafting effective captions is crucial for reels and videos alike. Here's how you can master the art:

- Keep it concise: Short captions are more likely to capture attention and keep viewers engaged.
- Incorporate keywords: Strategically insert relevant keywords to enhance discoverability through search engines and Instagram's algorithm.
- SEO-friendly approach: Optimize your captions with SEO in mind to attract targeted audiences and improve your content's visibility.
- Engage with intrigue: Create captions that intrigue and provoke curiosity, compelling users to stay on your page longer.

Remember, engaging captions not only please your audience but also signal to Instagram that your content is worth promoting to a wider audience.

Video: The Importance of Captions

Captions play a pivotal role in capturing and retaining viewer attention in the dynamic world of Instagram. Short, keyword-rich captions not only enhance discoverability but also encourage viewers to explore more of your content. As Instagram increasingly prioritizes SEO-friendly content, mastering your captions can significantly boost your reach and engagement metrics.

Effective Call to Action (CTA) Examples

Mastering the art of the Call to Action (CTA) can transform passive viewers into engaged followers. Here are some compelling CTA examples:

- Double-tap if you like what you see! Follow for more amazing content.
- Drop a comment below and let us know your thoughts!
- Share this video with a friend who needs to see it!
- Tag a friend who can relate to this!
- Swipe up to learn more or shop now!
- For more information, check out the link in our bio.
- Don't miss out! Sign up for our newsletter through the link in our bio.

These CTAs encourage interaction and deepen engagement, inviting your audience to take meaningful actions that benefit your content strategy.

Incorporating Effective CTAs
Utilizing effective CTAs in your content is pivotal for engaging your audience and inviting them to interact with your posts. These examples illustrate how strategic calls to action can prompt viewers to engage further with your content.

Keyword Research Essentials
To optimize your Instagram presence, mastering keyword research is key. Here's how you can effectively integrate keywords into your captions:

Identify relevant keywords: Make a list of keywords pertinent to your niche and target audience.
Use Google Keyword Planner: Leverage this tool to discover trending keywords and phrases that resonate with your audience.

Explore autocomplete suggestions: Google's autocomplete feature offers valuable insights into popular search queries related to your content.

By incorporating these keywords into your captions, you enhance your content's searchability and appeal to a broader audience on Instagram.

Leveraging Keyword Research

Keyword research is foundational for enhancing your content's visibility and appeal on Instagram. These steps outline how to strategically integrate keywords into your captions, optimizing your reach and engagement with precision.

The Significance of Hashtags

Harnessing the power of hashtags can amplify your content's reach and engagement. Here's how you can leverage hashtags effectively:

Use all 30 hashtags: Maximize your reach by utilizing Instagram's full quota of hashtags.

Tailor hashtags: Include a mix of small, medium, and large hashtags relevant to your content.

Strategic placement: Integrate hashtags seamlessly within your captions to maximize discoverability.

Effective hashtag usage enhances your content's visibility and engagement, crucial for organic growth and audience interaction.

Maximizing Hashtags

Hashtags are integral to enhancing your content's discoverability and engagement on Instagram. Discover how to strategically incorporate hashtags into your posts to expand your reach and foster meaningful interactions with your audience.

Crafting Compelling Captions

Crafting compelling captions is an art that involves balancing brevity with impact. Learn how to captivate your audience through well-crafted captions that resonate and encourage interaction.

This restructured content provides a comprehensive guide on captions, emphasizing their importance, effective use of keywords, crafting compelling CTAs, mastering hashtag strategies, and leveraging SEO to enhance content visibility and engagement on Instagram.

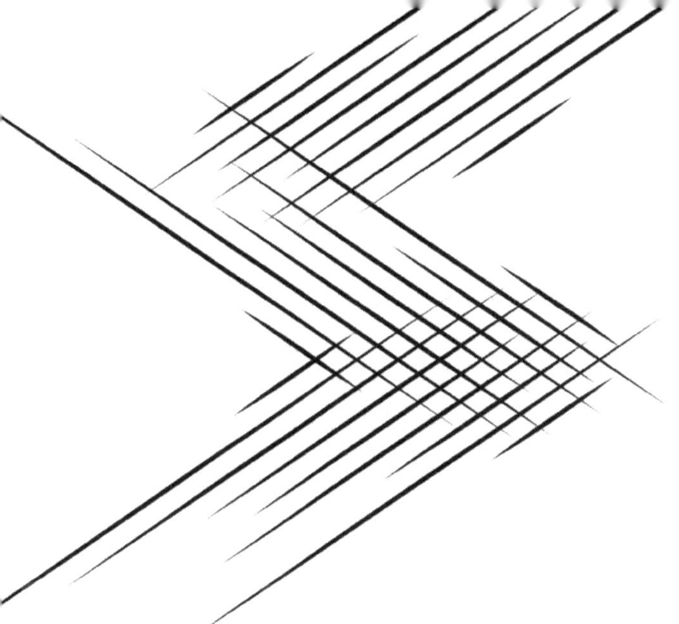

Batching Content for
Instagram Success

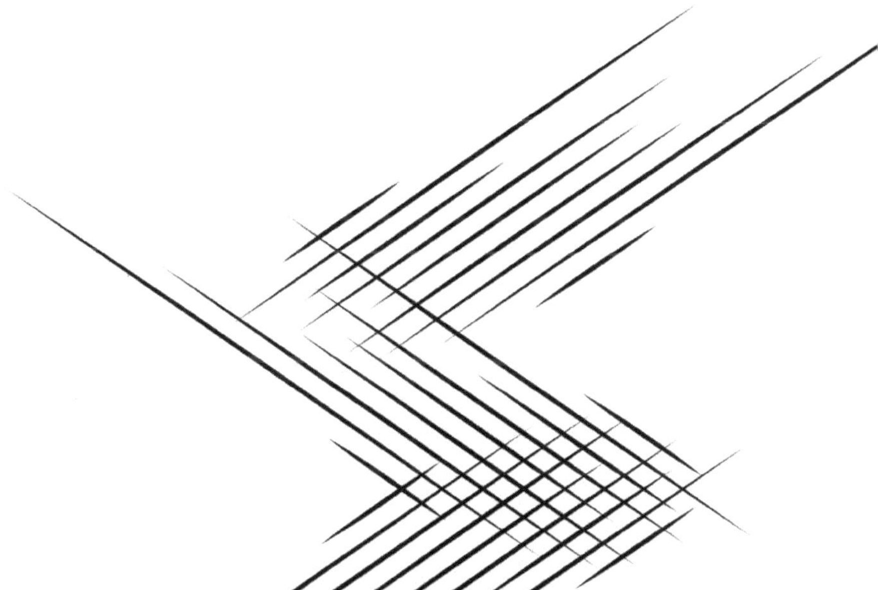

Batching Content for Instagram Success

Batching Content: A Strategic Approach
Batching content on Instagram is a powerful method to optimize your social media presence. By creating multiple pieces of content in one go and scheduling them for future release, you can streamline your workflow, maintain consistency, and effectively engage your audience. Here's how you can master the art of content batching:

Understanding Batching Content
Batching content on Instagram involves creating multiple pieces of content in a single session or over a short period, then scheduling or posting them at later dates. This method not only streamlines your content creation process but also ensures consistency and saves valuable time. It's an essential strategy for cultivating an engaging and well-organized Instagram profile.

Planning Your Batching Session
To effectively batch content for Instagram, start by setting clear objectives and themes for your upcoming content batch. Whether you aim to promote products, share educational content, or provide behind-the-scenes insights, defining your goals will guide your content creation process.

Creating a Content Calendar

Once you've established your content goals, create a content calendar outlining when and at what times you plan to post your batched content. This calendar serves as your roadmap, ensuring a cohesive and organized posting schedule that aligns with your overall Instagram strategy.

Preparing Your Resources

Gather all necessary resources for content creation in advance. This includes photos, videos, graphics, props, and any equipment needed for shooting. Having everything prepared beforehand minimizes interruptions during your batching session and ensures a seamless workflow.

Content Creation Session

Dedicate a focused session to shoot multiple pieces of content in one go. Choose a location and time when lighting and settings are consistent to maintain a cohesive visual style. Consider varying outfits or settings to add diversity to your content while maintaining your brand's aesthetic.

Crafting Captions and Hashtags

Write captions and select relevant hashtags for each piece of content in your batch. Crafting captions in advance allows you to concentrate on creativity and storytelling, enhancing the impact of your posts.

Utilize Instagram's scheduling tools or third-party platforms like Creator Studio, Buffer, or Hootsuite to schedule posts or save drafts for later release.

Engaging with Your Audience

Engage actively with your audience by responding to comments and messages promptly. Monitoring the performance of your batched content through engagement metrics enables you to gauge what resonates with your audience and refine your content strategy for future batches.

Continuous Improvement

Don't hesitate to experiment with different types of content within your batched posts. Each batch presents an opportunity to learn from analytics, refine your approach, and enhance your Instagram strategy over time.

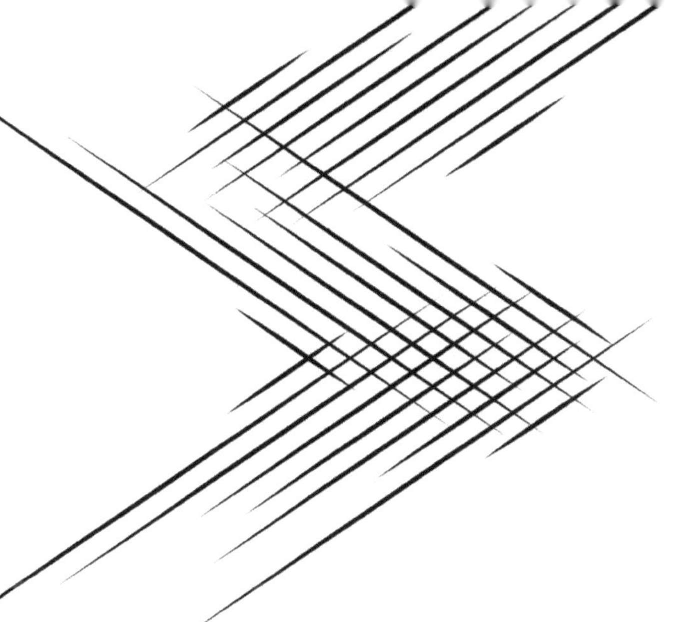

Mastering Reels:

Advanced Camera Techniques

Mastering Reels: Advanced Camera Techniques

Creating compelling Reels on Instagram requires more than just hitting record. It involves mastering advanced camera techniques that enhance your videos with professional quality and visual appeal. Whether you're an aspiring filmmaker or a social media enthusiast, these 18 advanced camera tips will elevate your Reels to the next level.

Mastering Reels with Advanced Camera Techniques

In the world of Instagram Reels, mastering advanced camera techniques is essential for creating content that stands out. From stabilizing your shots to experimenting with cinematic techniques, each tip is designed to help you achieve professional-quality videos that captivate your audience.

1. Use a Tripod or a Gimbal

Stabilize your shots by using a tripod or a smartphone gimbal. This eliminates shaky footage and ensures a polished, professional look.

2. Manual Focus and Exposure

Take control of your shots by manually adjusting focus and exposure settings. This allows you to manipulate depth of field and lighting for cinematic effects.

3. Frame Your Shots Thoughtfully

Pay attention to composition using techniques like the rule of thirds, leading lines, and framing to create visually appealing Reels.

4. Experiment with Different Lenses

Explore the capabilities of your smartphone's lenses (wide-angle, telephoto, etc.) to capture diverse perspectives and creative effects.

5. Shoot in Landscape Mode

Opt for landscape orientation (horizontal) to fill more of the screen and enhance visual appeal on most devices.

6. Use External Microphones

Enhance audio quality with external microphones such as Lavaliere or shotgun mics for clear and professional sound.

7. Adjust Frame Rate and Resolution

Experiment with different frame rates (24fps, 30fps, 60fps) and resolutions (1080p, 4K) to achieve cinematic motion or smooth playback.

8. Proper Lighting

Experiment with natural light, soft boxes, or ring lights to set the mood and eliminate harsh shadows for a polished look.

9. Time-Lapse and Slow-Motion

Utilize time-lapse and slow-motion modes in your camera app to create captivating visual sequences.

10. Manual White Balance

Adjust white balance settings to ensure accurate colors, especially in challenging lighting conditions.

11. Use ND Filters

Employ Neutral Density (ND) filters to control light intake, allowing for wider apertures or slower shutter speeds in bright environments.

12. Cinematic Focus Pulls

Create cinematic effects by manually adjusting focus during a shot (focus pull), adding depth and drama to your Reels.

13. Experiment with Cinematic Techniques

Explore advanced techniques like rack focusing, dolly zooms, and panning shots to infuse cinematic flair into your videos.

14. Colour Grading

Post-production, use video editing software to color grade your footage, achieving a distinct visual style for your Reels.

15. Storyboard Your Reel
Plan your Reel in advance with a storyboard to visualize necessary shots and structure, ensuring a cohesive narrative.

16. Record in High-Quality Audio
Ensure clear audio by using external microphones for recording in controlled environments with minimal background noise.

17. Dynamic Angles and Perspectives
Experiment with unique camera angles and perspectives to create visually stimulating Reels that engage viewers.

18. Edit for Impact
Fine-tune your Reels using video editing software to add transitions, text overlays, and music, enhancing the final product for maximum impact.

Mastering these advanced camera techniques will not only elevate the quality of your Instagram Reels but also distinguish your content in a crowded digital landscape. By integrating these tips into your creative process, you'll captivate your audience and establish a distinctive presence on Instagram.

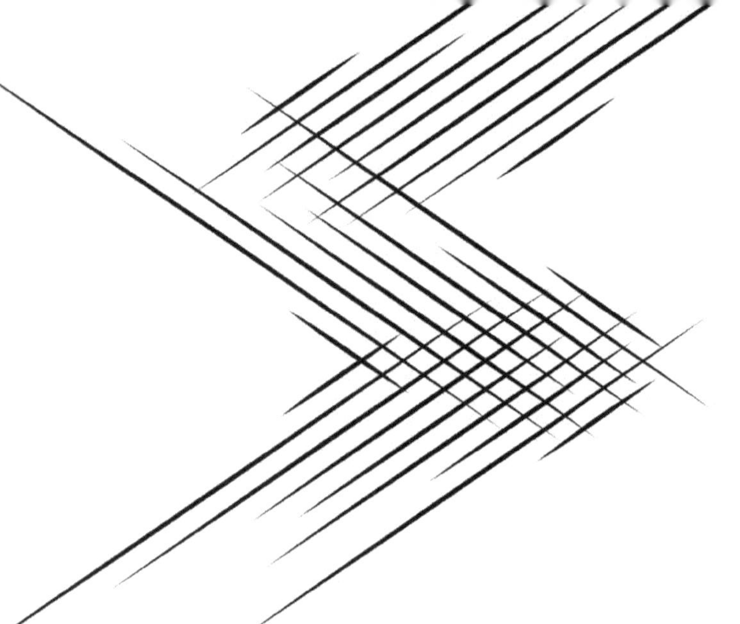

Mastering Reel Hooks: Strategies to Captivate Audiences

Mastering Reel Hooks: Strategies to Captivate Audiences

In the fast-paced world of Instagram Reels, capturing your audience's attention within seconds is crucial. Reel hooks are the secret sauce that not only grabs attention but also keeps viewers engaged throughout your video. These hooks leverage curiosity, intrigue, and a touch of urgency to draw viewers into your content, making them essential for a successful social media marketing strategy.

Mastering Reel Hooks: Strategies to Captivate Audiences

Mastering the art of Reel hooks is essential for anyone looking to stand out in the competitive landscape of Instagram. These hooks are designed to intrigue and captivate your audience from the very first second, ensuring they stay engaged with your content.

1. "Watch Till the End"

Encourage viewers to stick around by teasing them with intriguing snippets and promising a payoff at the end of the video.

2. Quick Hacks

Offer quick solutions or tips that promise to simplify your audience's lives, such as "One-minute hacks" or "5-minute crafts."

3. "How I Went From This to This"
Share transformation stories that showcase personal growth or significant changes, sparking curiosity about your journey.

4. "Are You Making This Mistake?"
Highlight common errors or misconceptions to pique curiosity and draw viewers who want to avoid pitfalls.

5. "If You're Making This Mistake, This Video Is for You"
Directly address your audience's pain points or challenges, promising solutions that keep them engaged till the end.

6. "Why Aren't You Talking About This?"
Pose intriguing questions that provoke thought and curiosity, prompting viewers to seek answers within your Reel.

7. "My Life/Business Changed With This"
Share impactful stories of transformation or success, showcasing the evolution of your journey or business.

8. "Five Things I Wish I Knew About..."
Educate your audience with valuable insights or information that they may not be aware of, positioning yourself as an expert.

9. "Three Ways I Increased... and You Can Too"

Offer actionable advice or strategies that promise tangible results, motivating viewers to learn and apply new skills.

10. "Try This New..."

Introduce new trends, products, or ideas that capture curiosity and encourage viewers to stay updated with your content.

11. "Stop Using..."

Educate your audience about harmful practices or habits, positioning your content as informative and authoritative.

12. "Top 5 Products for Glowing Skin"

Provide valuable recommendations that resonate with your audience's interests or needs, establishing credibility in your niche.

13. "Giveaway Contest"

Incentivize engagement with giveaways that encourage followers to participate and share your content, expanding your reach.

14. "Don't Try This at Home"

Create intrigue or humor by showcasing activities that are challenging or unconventional, prompting viewers to watch for entertainment or cautionary reasons.

15. "3 Things You Should Never Do in Your Life"
Offer thought-provoking insights or advice that resonates with viewers, positioning your Reels as must-watch content for valuable life lessons.

Mastering these 15 Reel hook ideas will transform your Instagram presence by capturing attention, boosting engagement, and expanding your audience reach. By strategically implementing these hooks into your content strategy, you'll create compelling Reels that resonate with viewers and elevate your social media influence.

Mastering Instagram:

Strategies for Engagement and Growth

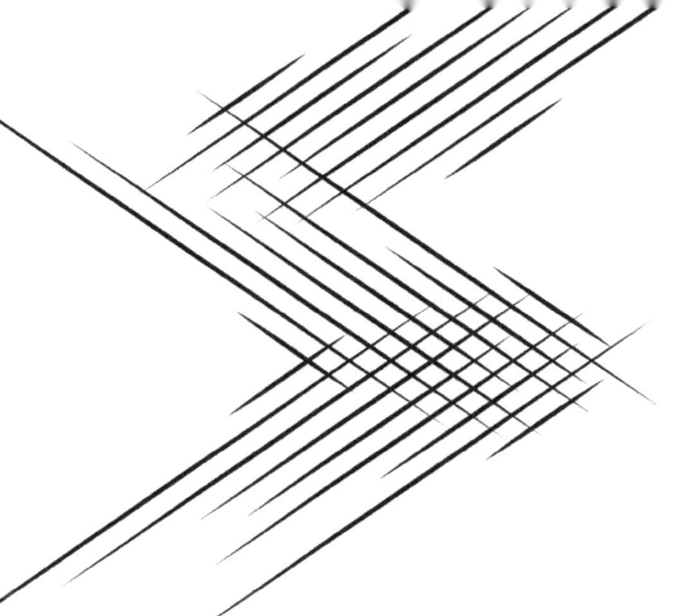

Mastering Instagram: Strategies for Engagement and Growth

In the dynamic realm of Instagram, mastering the right strategies can elevate your profile, engage your audience, and fuel growth. From leveraging the power of Reels to crafting compelling content, each element plays a crucial role in building a vibrant presence on the platform.

Mastering Instagram: Strategies for Engagement and Growth
Mastering Instagram requires a multifaceted approach that encompasses everything from captivating Reels to meaningful interactions with your audience. Here, we explore thirteen essential strategies to help you thrive on this influential platform.

1. Embrace the Rise of Reels
With Instagram prioritizing Reels, capitalize on this trend by creating niche-specific content that captivates your audience. Always include a call-to-action (CTA) to prompt engagement and broaden your reach efficiently.

2. Evolving Beyond the Feed
The traditional Instagram feed is no longer the primary focus. Instead, focus on delivering entertaining and valuable content that resonates with your audience's interests, regardless of feed aesthetics.

3. Deliver Value with Purpose

Adding value isn't just about sharing knowledge; it's about presenting content in a way that genuinely benefits your audience. Whether it's through detailed tutorials, product showcases, or insightful tips, prioritize content that enriches the viewer's experience.

4. Entertainment as a Priority

Entertainment is key to keeping your audience engaged. Whether through dance, humor, cooking, or creative skits, prioritize content that entertains and encourages repeat views.

5. Harnessing the Power of AI

Utilize AI tools like Upleap, Otter.ai, and Cortex to streamline content creation and analyze audience behavior. These tools save time and enhance efficiency, allowing you to focus more on engaging content creation.

6. Follower Dynamics: Quality over Quantity

Instead of fixating on follower counts, concentrate on fostering genuine connections with your audience. Analyze follower patterns to refine your content strategy continually.

7. Cultivate Positive Relationships

Maintain a respectful and responsive approach to audience interactions. Embrace constructive feedback and suggestions to build a loyal community around your content.

8. Elevate Video Content Quality

Enhance the quality of your Instagram videos, including Reels, IGTV, and live sessions. Engaging video content attracts and retains more viewers, driving higher engagement rates.

9. Storytelling through Stories

Use Instagram Stories strategically to deliver valuable, timely content. Incorporate trending topics and compelling CTAs to resonate with your audience's interests and increase interaction.

10. Collaborate for Growth

Collaborate with brands and fellow creators through various Instagram formats like Reels and carousel posts. Collaborations not only expand your reach but also provide insights into diverse audience demographics.

11. Engage with Carousel Posts

Utilize carousel posts to share detailed information, engaging narratives, and diverse content formats. These posts maximize engagement by catering to different viewing preferences.

12. Authenticity with Real-Life Content

Balance curated content with real-life moments to humanize your brand. Authenticity fosters deeper connections with your audience, who appreciate relatable and genuine content.

13. Audience-Centric Content Creation

Prioritize content that resonates with your audience's preferences and interests. Tailor your Reels and posts to captivate viewers within seconds, ensuring content relevance and viewer retention.

By mastering these thirteen strategies, you'll optimize your Instagram presence for engagement, growth, and sustained audience interest. Implementing these insights will not only elevate your content but also strengthen your influence within the vibrant Instagram community.

Mastering the Instagram Algorithm:

Proven Strategies for Growth

Mastering the Instagram Algorithm: Proven Strategies for Growth

Mastering the Instagram algorithm isn't just about luck—it's about leveraging proven strategies to enhance visibility, engagement, and ultimately, success. Join me as we delve into six powerful strategies to hack the Instagram algorithm and amplify your presence on this influential platform.

Strategy 1: Pique Interest

Instagram thrives on user engagement and interests. To captivate your audience, create content that offers value, incorporates strong calls-to-action (CTAs), and showcases your expertise. Videos and carousels are algorithm favorites—use them to engage your audience deeply.

Strategy 2: Timing is Key

Consistency in posting is crucial. Understand your audience's habits and post at optimal times. Commit to a posting schedule for at least three months to build momentum and maximize engagement.

Strategy 3: Embrace New Features

Stay ahead by embracing Instagram's latest features like IGTV and Reels. These features are prioritized by the algorithm, offering prime opportunities for increased visibility and discovery.

Strategy 4: Harness the Power of Hashtags

Hashtags remain potent tools for categorizing content and reaching targeted audiences. Use relevant, trending hashtags wisely—stick to a maximum of 20 per post to avoid diluting your content's impact.

Strategy 5: Engage with Your Community

Build relationships with your audience and industry peers. Engage with followers, competitors, and influencers in your niche. This interaction signals relevance to the algorithm, boosting your content's reach.

Strategy 6: Leverage Brand Interactions

Interact authentically with prominent brands in your niche. Leave insightful comments on their posts to increase visibility among their followers—a strategy that can lead to valuable partnerships and expanded reach.

Pro Tips for Maximizing Engagement

Encourage followers to turn on notifications to stay updated on your content. Remind them periodically, as this can significantly enhance engagement. Avoid auto-scheduling posts to mitigate technical issues that may impact reach.

By implementing these six strategies, you'll not only decode the Instagram algorithm but also position yourself for sustained growth and engagement. Let's harness the power of these insights to elevate your Instagram presence and achieve lasting impact in the digital realm.

Congratulations on completing this journey towards Instagram mastery! Remember, success on this platform is not just about followers or likes, but about creating genuine connections and sharing your unique story with the world.

Keep experimenting, stay authentic, and adapt to the ever-changing landscape of social media. Your dedication and creativity will open doors to new opportunities and collaborations. Now, go forth and turn your Instagram dreams into reality. The world is ready to see what you have to offer!

For any doubts or knowledge sharing, you can reach me out at grtguru@gmail.com